# Teach Yourself VISUALLY™

# iPod touch®

**Visual**™

## Guy Hart-Davis

WILEY

John Wiley & Sons, Inc.

## Teach Yourself VISUALLY™ iPod touch®

Published by
**John Wiley & Sons, Inc.**
10475 Crosspoint Boulevard
Indianapolis, IN 46256

www.wiley.com

Published simultaneously in Canada

Wiley publishes in a variety of print and electronic formats and by print-on-demand. Some material included with standard print versions of this book may not be included in e-books or in print-on-demand. If this book refers to media such as a CD or DVD that is not included in the version you purchased, you may download this material at http://booksupport.wiley.com. For more information about Wiley products, visit www.wiley.com.

Library of Congress Control Number: 2012954232

ISBN: 978-1-118-51044-5

Manufactured in the United States of America

10 9 8 7 6 5 4 3 2 1

### Trademark Acknowledgments

### Contact Us

For general information on our other products and services please contact our Customer Care Department within the U.S. at 877-762-2974, outside the U.S. at 317-572-3993 or fax 317-572-4002.

For technical support please visit www.wiley.com/techsupport.

**WILEY**   Sales | Contact Wiley at (877) 762-2974 or fax (317) 572-4002.

# Credits

**Acquisitions Editor**
Aaron Black

**Sr. Project Editor**
Sarah Hellert

**Technical Editor**
Dennis R. Cohen

**Copy Editors**
Gwenette Gaddis
Scott Tullis
Marylouise Wiack

**Editorial Director**
Robyn Siesky

**Business Manager**
Amy Knies

**Sr. Marketing Manager**
Sandy Smith

**Vice President and Executive
Group Publisher**
Richard Swadley

**Vice President and Executive
Publisher**
Barry Pruett

**Project Coordinator**
Katie Crocker

**Graphics and Production Specialists**
Ronda David-Burroughs
Noah Hart
Jennifer Henry
Jennifer Mayberry

**Quality Control Technician**
Lindsay Amones

**Proofreader**
Wordsmith Editorial

**Indexer**
Potomac Indexing, LLC

## About the Author

**Guy Hart-Davis** is the author of *Teach Yourself VISUALLY iPhone 5*, *Teach Yourself VISUALLY Mac mini*, *Teach Yourself VISUALLY iMac*, 2nd Edition, *iMac Portable Genius*, 4th Edition, *iLife '11 Portable Genius*, and *iWork '09 Portable Genius*.

## Author's Acknowledgments

My thanks go to the many people who turned my manuscript into the highly graphical book you are holding. In particular, I thank Aaron Black for asking me to write the book; Sarah Hellert for keeping me on track and guiding the editorial process; Gwenette Gaddis, Scott Tullis, and Marylouise Wiack for skillfully editing the text; Dennis Cohen for reviewing the book for technical accuracy and contributing helpful suggestions; and Ronda David-Burroughs and Noah Hart for creating the pictures.

# How to Use This Book

## Who This Book Is For

This book is for the reader who has never used this particular technology or software application. It is also for readers who want to expand their knowledge.

## The Conventions in This Book

### ① Steps

This book uses a step-by-step format to guide you easily through each task. **Numbered steps** are actions you must do; **bulleted steps** clarify a point, step, or optional feature; and **indented steps** give you the result.

### ② Notes

Notes give additional information — special conditions that may occur during an operation, a situation that you want to avoid, or a cross-reference to a related area of the book.

### ③ Icons and Buttons

Icons and buttons show you exactly what you need to click to perform a step.

### ④ Tips

Tips offer additional information, including warnings and shortcuts.

### ⑤ Bold

**Bold** type shows command names or options that you must click or text or numbers you must type.

### ⑥ Italics

*Italic* type introduces and defines a new term.

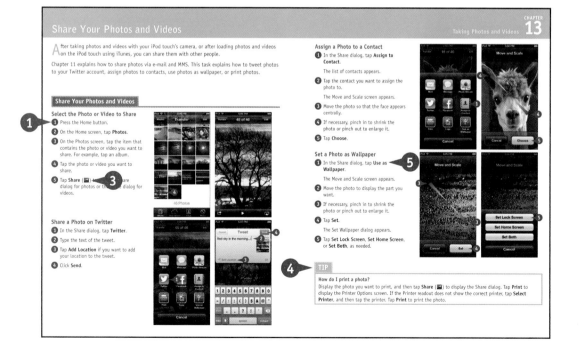

# Table of Contents

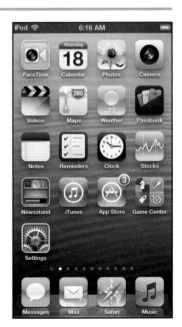

## Chapter 3   Personalizing Your iPod touch

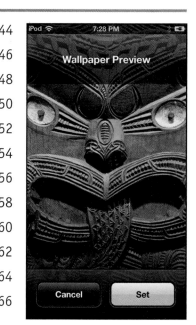

## Chapter 4   Working with Siri and Dictation

# Table of Contents

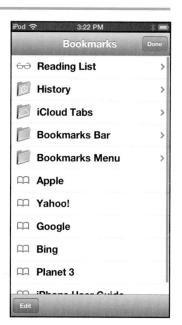

# Table of Contents

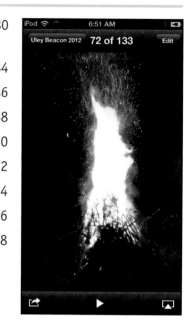

# Table of Contents

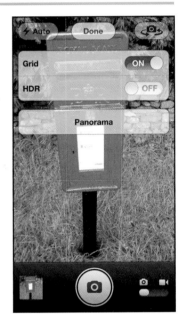

## Chapter 14 Advanced Features and Troubleshooting

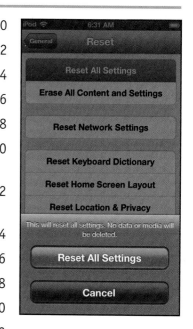

# CHAPTER 1

# Getting Started with Your iPod touch

In this chapter, you set up your iPod touch to work with your computer or iCloud and choose items to sync.

# Unbox the iPod touch and Charge It

O nce you have gotten your iPod touch, your first move is to unbox it, identify the components, and set the iPod touch to charge.

To get the best battery life out of your iPod touch, you should first fully charge the battery, even if it came partly charged. So no matter how eager you are to set up your iPod touch, sync it with iTunes or iCloud, and start using it, take a few hours to charge it fully first.

## Unbox the iPod touch and Charge It

**1** Open the iPod touch's box, and remove its contents.

**2** Make sure you have the iPod touch itself and the following components:

**A** The EarPods headset.

**B** The USB-to-Lightning cable.

**C** The iPod touch loop.

**3** Peel the protective stickers off the front and back of the iPod touch.

**4** Connect the USB end of the USB cable to a USB port on your computer.

**Note:** Make sure that the USB port provides enough power to the iPod touch. Some USB ports on keyboards, other external devices, and even some older computers do not provide enough.

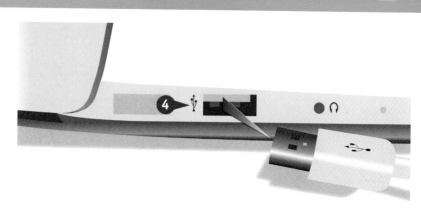

**5** Connect the Lightning connector end of the USB cable to the iPod touch.

**Note:** The connector is reversible, so you can plug it in either way up.

A Charging readout appears on-screen.

**6** Leave the iPod touch to charge until the battery readout shows that the battery is fully charged.

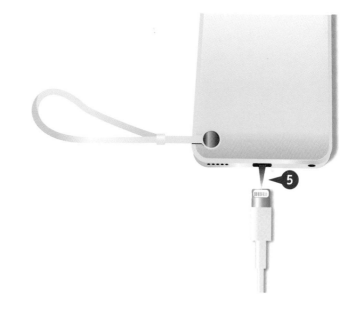

## TIP

**Can I charge the iPod touch using a power adapter instead of using my computer?**

Yes. If you buy the Apple USB Power Adapter or a third-party equivalent adapter, you can charge your iPod touch by using the power adapter. This is especially useful if you do not have a computer.

# Turn On the iPod touch and Meet the Hardware Controls

After charging your iPod touch, turn it on and meet its hardware controls. For essential actions, such as turning on and controlling volume, the iPod touch has a Power/Sleep button, a Volume Up button and a Volume Down button, together with the Home button below the screen.


## Turn On the iPod touch and Meet the Hardware Controls

1 Press and hold the Power/ Sleep button on top of the iPod touch for a couple of seconds.

As the iPod touch starts, the Apple logo appears on the screen.

Ⓐ Above the iPod touch's screen is the front-facing camera.

Ⓑ Below the iPod touch's screen is the Home button, which you press to display the Home screen.

At the bottom of the iPod touch are:

Ⓒ The headphone socket.

Ⓓ The Lightning connector.

Ⓔ The speaker.

**2** Turn the iPod touch so that you can see its left side.

**3** Press the Volume Up (+) button to increase the ringer volume.

**4** Press the Volume Down (–) button to decrease the ringer volume.

**5** When the lock screen appears, tap the **slide to unlock** slider, and then drag your finger to the right.

The iPod touch unlocks, and the Home screen appears.

**Note:** The iPod touch can play ringtones to alert you to incoming FaceTime calls and other tones to alert you to other events, such as the arrival of instant messages or the reminders for calendar appointments.

---

**TIP**

**Do the hardware controls have other uses than those discussed here?**

Yes. Apart from the primary uses, the hardware controls have the following extra uses:

- Power/Sleep button. If your iPod touch becomes unresponsive, you can hold down this button to restart it.

- Volume Up (+) button. When the insertion point is displaying the Camera app, press this button to take a picture.

- Home button. Press this button twice in rapid succession to display the recently used apps bar across the bottom of the screen.

# Download, Install, and Set Up iTunes

To sync your iPod touch with your computer, you use Apple's iTunes application. iTunes comes preinstalled on every Mac but not on PCs; to get iTunes for Windows, you download it from the Apple website and then install it on your PC.

If you do not have a computer, or you do not want to sync your iPod touch with your computer, you can set up and sync your iPod touch using Apple's iCloud service, as described later in this chapter.

## Download, Install, and Set Up iTunes

**1** On your PC, open the web browser, Internet Explorer in this example.

**2** Click the Address box, type **www. apple.com/itunes/download**, and then press **Enter**.

The Download iTunes Now web page appears.

**3** Deselect the check boxes (☑ changes to ☐) unless you want to receive e-mail from Apple.

**4** Click **Download Now**.

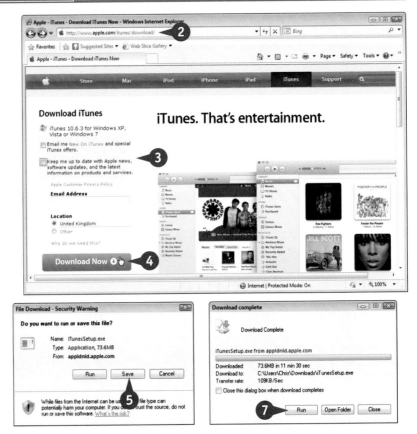

The File Download – Security Warning dialog opens.

**5** Click **Save**.

The Save As dialog appears.

**6** Select the download location — for example, your Downloads folder — and then click **Save**.

The download starts.

**7** In the Download Complete dialog, click **Run**.

The iTunes Installer opens.

**8** Click **Next**, and then follow the steps of the installer.

**Note:** You must accept the license agreement in order to install iTunes. On the Installation Options screen, click the **Add iTunes and QuickTime shortcuts to my desktop** check box (☑ changes to ☐) unless you need these shortcuts.

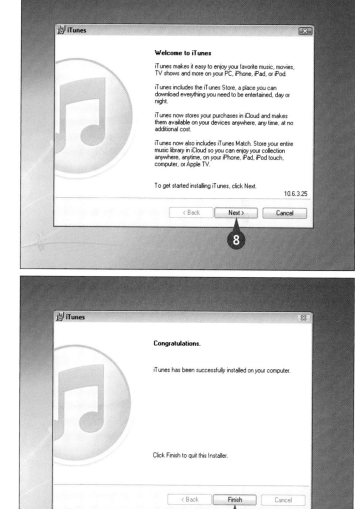

When the installation finishes, the installer displays the Congratulations screen.

**9** Click **Finish**.

The installer closes.

**10** If the installer prompts you to restart your PC, restart it as soon as is convenient.

**How do I set up iTunes on a Mac?**

If you have not run iTunes already, click the **iTunes** icon (⊙) that appears on the Dock by default. If the Dock contains no iTunes icon, click **Launchpad** (⊙) on the Dock, and then click **iTunes** (⊙) on the Launchpad screen. The iTunes Setup Assistant launches. Follow the steps to set up iTunes.

# Set Up Your iPod touch Using iTunes

Before you can use your iPod touch, you must set it up. You can set up the iPod touch through iTunes, as described in this task, or by using iCloud, as explained later in this chapter.

During setup, you can make broad choices about which items to sync automatically with the iPod touch. You can choose other sync options as described in the next task.

## Set Up Your iPod touch Using iTunes

**1** Turn on the iPod touch by pressing and holding the Power/Sleep button for a couple of seconds until the Apple logo appears on-screen.

**2** When the initial iPod screen appears, tap the slider and drag it to the right.

The iPod touch unlocks and begins the setup routine.

**3** If the Language screen shows the language you want to use, tap **Next**. Otherwise, tap **Show More**, tap the language on the screen that appears, and then tap ➡.

**4** If the first Country or Region screen shows the correct country or region, tap **Next**. Otherwise, tap **Show More**, tap the country or region on the second Country or Region screen, and then tap **Next**.

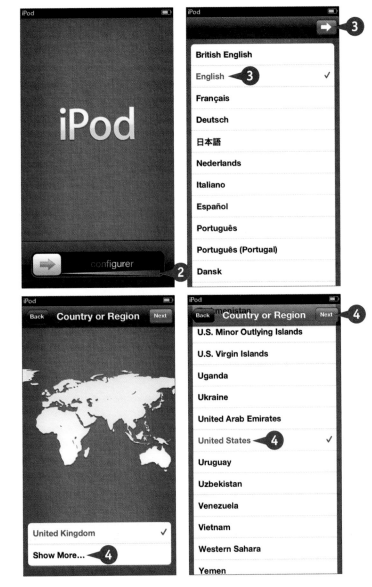

The Wi-Fi screen appears.

**5** Tap **Connect to iTunes**.

**6** Connect your iPod touch to your computer using the USB cable.

The iTunes window appears.

**7** On the Set Up Your iPod screen, change the name as needed.

**8** Select **Automatically sync songs and videos to my iPod** (☐ changes to ☑) to sync songs and videos.

**Note:** To control which items you sync, deselect this check box (☑ changes to ☐) and see the next task.

**9** Select **Automatically add photos to my iPod** (☐ changes to ☑) if you want to sync photos automatically.

**10** Select **Automatically sync apps to my iPod** (☐ changes to ☑) to sync new apps automatically. Syncing apps automatically is usually helpful.

**11** Click **Done**.

iTunes syncs your iPod touch.

**What should I do if iTunes does not open when I connect my iPod touch?**

If iTunes does not open automatically, launch iTunes manually. In OS X, click **iTunes** (🎵) on the Dock or in the Applications folder. In Windows, click **Start** and then **iTunes**.

# Choose Which Items to Sync

After setting up your iPod touch, you can choose which items to sync to it. You can sync a wide range of items, ranging from your contacts, calendars, and e-mail accounts to your music, movies, books, and photos. This task shows you how to sync the items you will most likely need at first: contacts, calendars, e-mail, music, movies, and photos. This task shows OS X screens; the Windows screens are similar, but some items have different names.

## Choose Which Items to Sync

**1** Connect your iPod touch to your computer.

The iTunes window appears.

**2** Click your iPod touch.

**Note:** Your iPod touch appears in iTunes with the name you gave it.

The iPod touch's control screens appear.

**3** Click **Info**.

The Info tab appears.

**4** Click **Sync Contacts** (☐ changes to ☑) if you want to sync contacts.

**Note:** In Windows, you can sync contacts from Windows Contacts, Google Contacts, Outlook, or Yahoo! Contacts. You can sync calendars with Outlook.

**5** Choose which contacts to sync. For example, click **All contacts** (○ changes to ●).

**6** Click **Sync Calendars** (☐ changes to ☑) if you want to sync calendars.

**7** Choose which calendars to sync. For example, click **Selected calendars** (○ changes to ●) and then click the check box (☐ changes to ☑) for each calendar to sync.

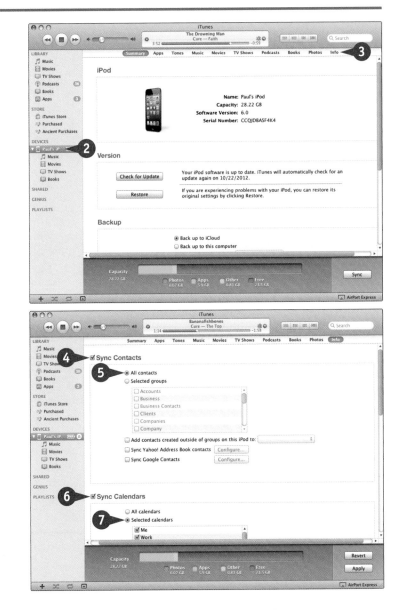

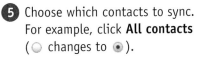

**8** Click **Sync Mail Accounts** (☐ changes to ☑) if you want to sync e-mail accounts. Then click the check box (☐ changes to ☑) for each e-mail account to sync.

**9** Click **Sync Safari bookmarks** (☐ changes to ☑) if you want to sync bookmarks.

**Note:** In Windows, you can sync e-mail from Outlook or Outlook Express. You can sync bookmarks from Internet Explorer or Safari.

**10** Click **Apps**.

The Apps tab appears.

**11** Click **Sync Apps** (☐ changes to ☑).

**12** Select the check box for each app you want to sync to the iPod touch.

**13** Scroll down the screen and select **Automatically sync new apps** (☐ changes to ☑) if you want to sync new apps automatically. This is usually helpful.

**14** Click **Music**.

---

**TIP**

**Should I sync my entire music library to my iPod touch?**
This depends on how big your music library is, how high your iPod touch's capacity is, and how much other data you need to put on the iPod touch. In iTunes, click **Music** in the left column, and then click **All** in the Genres box, **All** in the Artist box, and **All** in the Albums box. The readout at the bottom of the iTunes window shows you how much space the items occupy, enabling you to judge whether they will all fit on the iPod touch.

continued ▶

When you have chosen all the items to sync, you click the **Apply** button to run the sync. The initial sync normally takes much longer than subsequent syncs — often several hours or even overnight. This is because iTunes must transfer large amounts of data, such as your music files, to the iPod touch. Subsequent syncs typically involve much less data, so they go much faster.

## Choose Which Items to Sync (continued)

The Music tab appears.

 Click **Sync Music** (☐ changes to ☑).

 Use the controls in the Sync Music box, Playlists box, Artists box, Genres box, and Albums box to specify which music to sync.

Ⓐ Click **Automatically fill free space with songs** (☐ changes to ☑) if you want to put as much music as possible on your iPod touch.

⑰ Click **Movies**.

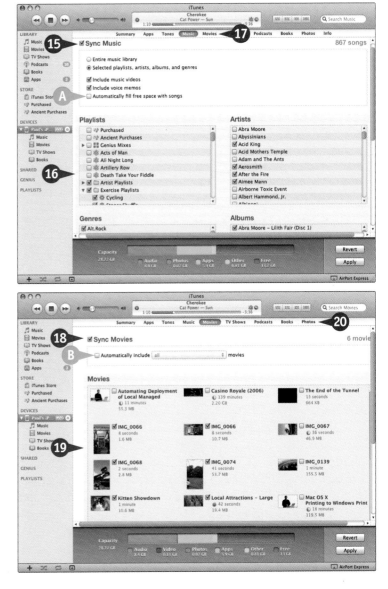

The Movies tab appears.

⑱ Click **Sync Movies** (☐ changes to ☑).

⑲ Choose which movies to sync.

Ⓑ To sync only movies you have not watched, click **Automatically include** (☐ changes to ☑), open the pop-up menu, and choose a suitable setting — for example, **5 most recent unwatched** movies.

⑳ Click **Photos**.

The Photos tab appears.

**21** Click **Sync Photos from** ( ☐ changes to ☑ ).

**Note:** In Windows, click **Sync Photos with** ( ☐ changes to ☑ ), and then choose the folder in the drop-down list.

**22** In the pop-up menu, choose the source of the photos — for example, iPhoto.

**23** Choose which photos to sync. For example, click **Selected albums, Events, and Faces, and automatically include** ( ○ changes to ◉ ), and then choose which albums, events, and faces to include.

**24** Click **Apply**.

iTunes syncs the items to your iPod touch.

**C** The readout shows you the sync progress.

**D** If you need to stop the sync, click ⊗.

**25** When the sync finishes, disconnect your iPod touch.

TIP

**How do I sync ringtones, TV shows, podcasts, and books?**
To sync ringtones, TV shows, podcasts, and books, click the appropriate tab in iTunes, and then use the controls to specify which items you want. For example, for TV shows, you can click **Sync TV Shows** ( ☐ changes to ☑ ) and then choose a setting such as **Automatically include the 3 newest unwatched episodes of all shows**.

# Sync Your iPod touch with iTunes via Wi-Fi

The normal way to sync your iPod touch with iTunes is by using the USB cable to connect the iPod touch to your computer. But if you connect both your computer and your iPod touch to the same network, you can sync the iPod touch with iTunes wirelessly. This is called syncing "over the air."

To use wireless sync, you must first enable it in iTunes. You can then have the iPod touch sync automatically when it is connected to a power source and to the same wireless network as the computer. You can also start a sync manually from the iPod touch, even if it is not connected to a power source.

## Sync Your iPod touch with iTunes via Wi-Fi

### Set Your iPod touch to Sync with iTunes via Wi-Fi

**1** Connect your iPod touch to your computer with the USB cable.

The iTunes window appears.

**2** Click your iPod touch.

**Note:** Your iPod touch appears in iTunes with the name you gave it.

The iPod touch's control screens appear.

**3** Click **Summary**.

The Summary tab appears.

**4** Click **Sync with this iPod over Wi-Fi** (☐ changes to ☑).

**5** Click **Apply**.

iTunes applies the change.

**6** Disconnect your iPod touch from your computer.

### Perform a Manual Sync via Wi-Fi

**1** Press the Home button.

The Home screen appears.

**2** Tap **Settings**.

The Settings screen appears.

**3** Tap **General**.

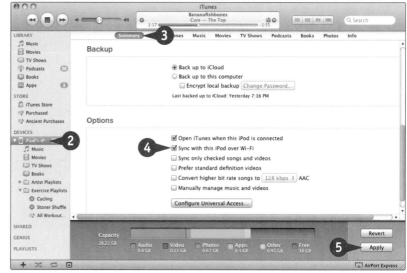

The General screen appears.

④ Tap **iTunes Wi-Fi Sync**.

The iTunes Wi-Fi Sync screen appears.

⑤ Tap **Sync Now**.

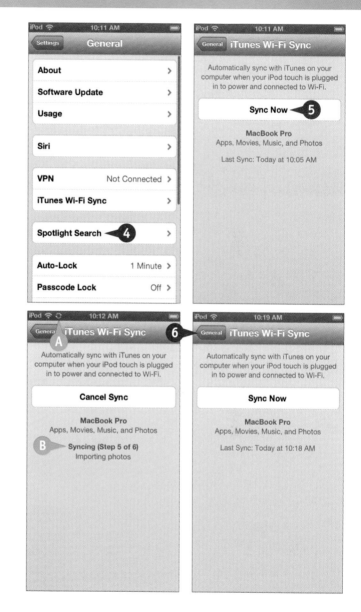

The sync runs.

Ⓐ The Sync symbol (⊘) appears in the status bar.

Ⓑ The readout shows which part of the sync is currently running.

⑥ When the sync completes, tap **General**.

The General screen appears again.

TIP

**Can I sync my iPod touch automatically via Wi-Fi?**

To sync your iPod touch automatically via Wi-Fi, connect your iPod touch to a power source — for example, the Apple USB Power Adapter. Make sure your computer is on and connected to your network, and that iTunes is running. Your iPod touch automatically connects to your computer across the wireless network. iTunes syncs the latest songs, videos, and data.

# Set Up Your iPod touch Using iCloud

Instead of using iTunes and your computer to set up and sync your iPod touch, you can set it up and sync it without a computer using Apple's iCloud online service. To do this, you need an Apple ID. You can create an Apple ID using either your existing e-mail address or a new iCloud account that you create during setup.

## Set Up Your iPod touch Using iCloud

**1** Follow steps **1** to **4** of the task "Set Up Your iPod touch Using iTunes" to begin setting up your iPod touch.

**2** On the Wi-Fi screen, tap your wireless network.

The Enter Password screen appears.

**3** Type the password.

**4** Tap **Join**.

The Wi-Fi screen appears again.

**5** Tap **Next**.

The Location Services screen appears.

**6** Tap **Enable Location Services** or **Disable Location Services**, as appropriate.

**7** Tap **Next**.

The Set Up iPod touch screen appears.

**8** Tap **Set Up as New iPod touch**.

**9** Tap **Next**.

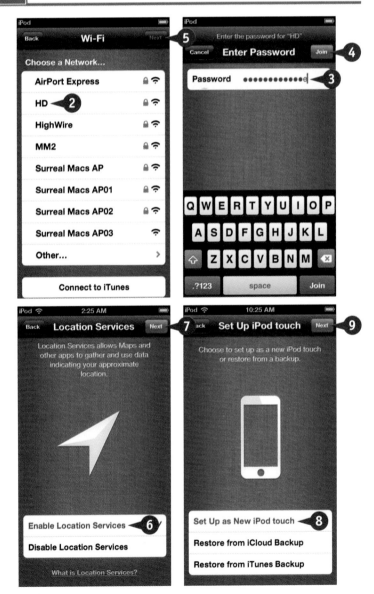

The Apple ID screen appears.

**10** Tap **Create a Free Apple ID**.

The Birthday screen appears.

**11** Move the spin wheels to your birthday or the date you want to claim is your birthday.

**12** Tap **Next**.

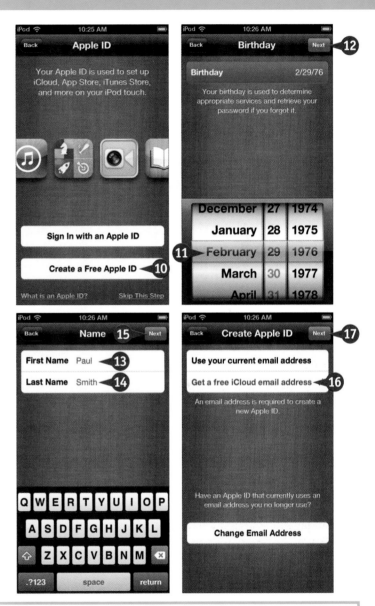

The Name screen appears.

**13** Tap the First Name box and type your first name.

**14** Tap the Last Name box and type your last name.

**15** Tap **Next**.

The Create Apple ID screen appears.

**16** Tap **Get a free iCloud email address**.

**17** Tap **Next**.

## TIP

**Should I sync my iPod touch with iCloud rather than with my computer?**

If you have a main computer that you use most of the time, you will probably be better off syncing your iPod touch with the computer than with iCloud. You can keep all your music and videos on your computer, organize them with iTunes, and then sync the items you want with your iPod touch, as discussed earlier in this chapter.

If you do not have a computer you use regularly, sync with iCloud. For example, if you use an iPad as your main computer, you must sync your iPod touch with iCloud because you cannot sync the iPod touch directly with the iPad.

**B**y using iCloud, you can synchronize your songs, videos, apps, and documents with other devices running Apple's iOS operating system. For example, if you have an iPad or an iPhone, you can use iCloud sync to keep that device's contents synced with your iPod touch's contents, and vice versa.

## Set Up Your iPod touch Using iCloud (continued)

The iCloud Email screen appears.

**18** Type the address you want to use.

**19** Tap **Next**.

The Apple ID Password screen appears.

**20** Type your password twice.

**21** Tap **Next**.

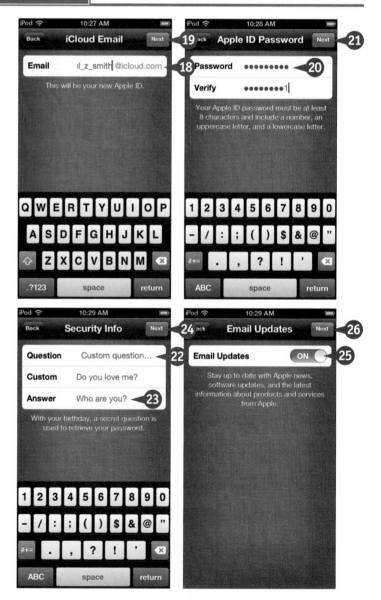

The Security Info screen appears.

**22** Tap the question you want to use. You can use a custom question for added security.

**23** Tap the Answer box, and type the answer to your question.

**24** Tap **Next**.

The Email Updates screen appears.

**25** Tap the **Email Updates** switch, and move it to Off if you do not want to receive e-mail updates from Apple.

**26** Tap **Next**.

27 Read the terms and conditions, and then tap **Agree**.

28 In the Terms and Conditions dialog, tap **Agree**.

29 On the Set Up iCloud screen, tap **Use iCloud**.

30 Tap **Next**.

31 On the iCloud Backup screen, tap **Back Up to iCloud**.

32 Tap **Next**.

33 On the Find My iPod touch screen, tap **Use Find My iPod touch**.

34 Tap **Next**.

35 On the Siri screen, tap **Use Siri** or **Don't Use Siri**, as needed.

36 Tap **Next**.

37 On the Diagnostics screen, tap the **Send Diagnostics** switch, and then tap **Automatically Send** or **Don't Send**, as appropriate.

38 Tap **Next**.

39 On the Thank You screen, tap **Start Using iPod touch**.

The Home screen appears, and you can start using the iPod touch, as discussed in the following task.

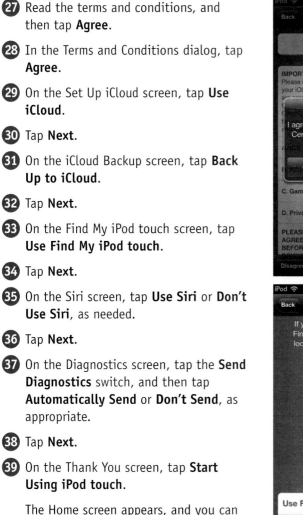

TIP

**Should I use the Find My iPod touch feature, or is it a threat to my privacy?**
The Find My iPod touch feature can help you locate your iPod touch if you have mislaid it or if someone has removed it. To use Find My iPod touch, you log in to iCloud using your Apple ID. You can then give the command to locate your iPod touch. Unless you share your Apple ID with others, no one but you can use Find My iPod touch, so it is not a privacy threat worth worrying about.

# Explore the iPod touch's User Interface and Launch Apps

After you sync the iPod touch or set it up with iCloud, you are ready to start using the iPod touch. When you press the Home button to wake the iPod touch from sleep, it displays the lock screen. You then unlock the iPod touch to reach the Home screen, which contains icons for running the apps installed on the iPod touch.

You can quickly launch an app by tapping its icon on the Home screen. From the app, you can return to the Home screen by pressing the Home button. You can then launch another app as needed.

## Explore the iPod touch's User Interface and Launch Apps

**1** Press the Home button.

The iPod touch's screen lights up and shows the Lock screen.

**2** Tap the slider and drag it to the right.

The iPod touch unlocks, and the Home screen appears.

**A** The iPod touch has two or more Home screens, depending on how many apps are installed. The gray dots at the bottom of the Home screen show how many Home screens there are. The white dot shows the current Home screen. The leftmost item in the row of dots is a magnifying glass representing Spotlight, the search feature.

**3** Tap **Notes**.

The Notes app opens.

**Note:** If you chose to sync notes with your iPod touch, the synced notes appear in the Notes app. Otherwise, the list is empty until you create a note.

**4** Tap **New** (⊞).

A new note opens, and the on-screen keyboard appears.

**5** Type a short note by tapping the keys.

**B** If a pop-up bubble suggests a correction, tap **space** to accept it. Tap × on the bubble to reject it.

**6** Tap **Done**.

The on-screen keyboard closes.

**7** Tap **Notes**.

**C** The Notes list appears, with your note in it.

**8** Press the Home button.

The Home screen appears.

**9** Tap and drag to the left to display the second Home screen.

**Note:** You can also tap at the right end of the row of dots on the Home screen to move one screen to the right. Tap at the left end to move one screen to the left.

You can now launch another app by tapping its icon.

**10** Press the Power/Sleep button.

Your iPod touch goes to sleep.

# Use Notification Center

As your communications hub, your iPod touch handles many different types of alerts for you: missed FaceTime calls, text messages, reminders, meetings, and so on.

To help you keep on top of all these alerts, your iPod touch integrates them into Notification Center, together with information about the current weather and stock prices. You can quickly access Notification Center from the Home screen or any other screen. After you display Notification Center, you can respond to an alert, view the weather, or check your current stock prices.

## Use Notification Center

### Open Notification Center

**1** When an alert appears at the top of the screen you are working on, tap the alert bar and drag it downward.

Notification Center appears.

**Note:** To clear all the notifications from a particular category in Notification Center, tap × at the right end of the category head, and then tap **Clear**, the button that appears in place of ×.

### View a Notification from Notification Center

**1** In Notification Center, tap the notification you want to see.

Notification Center displays the notification in its app.

**2** You can now work with the notification as needed. For example, you can reply to an instant message.

## Open the Weather App from Notification Center

1 In Notification Center, tap the weather item at the top of the screen.

The Weather app opens, displaying the current weather.

You can then swipe your finger to the left or right to view the weather for another location.

## Open the Stocks App from Notification Center

1 In Notification Center, tap the Stocks item at the bottom of the screen.

The Stocks app opens, displaying the current stock prices, market capitalizations, and charts.

**Note:** Tap at the bottom of the screen and drag your finger upward to close Notification Center.

**What happens if I receive a notification when my iPod touch is locked?**

What happens when you receive a notification while the screen is locked depends on the type of notification. For most types of notifications, your iPod touch displays an alert on the lock screen to alert you to the notification. Unlocking your iPod touch while the alert is displayed takes you directly to the notification in whatever app it belongs to — for example, to an instant message in the Messages app.

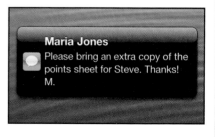

# CHAPTER 2

# Choosing Which Data to Sync

In this chapter, you learn to sync your contacts, calendars, mail accounts, notes, and other essential data with your iPod touch using iTunes. You also learn to put photos, books, and audiobooks on the iPod touch, and to transfer other types of files to the iPod touch using the iTunes File Sharing feature.

# Sync Contacts with Your iPod touch

To put your contacts on the iPod touch, you can sync them from your PC or Mac. iTunes and the iPod touch then keep the contacts synced, so that when you change contact information on one device, the changes appear on the other as well. You can choose between syncing all your contacts and syncing only particular groups — for example, only family and friends.

If you have an iCloud account and use it to sync your contacts with your iPod touch, do not also synchronize them as described here. If you do, you may get duplicated contacts on the iPod touch.

## Sync Contacts with Your iPod touch

1 Connect the iPod touch to your PC or Mac via USB or Wi-Fi.

2 In iTunes, click your iPod touch.

3 Click **Info**.

4 Click **Sync Contacts** (☐ changes to ☑).

**Note:** In Windows, click **Sync contacts with** (☐ changes to ☑). Then select the program that contains the contacts — for example, Outlook.

5 To sync only some contacts, click **Selected groups** (○ changes to ◉).

6 Click the check box for each contacts group you want to sync (☐ changes to ☑).

7 Click **Add contacts created outside of groups on this iPod to** (☐ changes to ☑).

8 Click ⬍ and then click the contacts group to which you want to add contacts created outside the iPod touch.

9 If you need to sync Yahoo! contacts, click **Sync Yahoo! Address Book contacts** (☐ changes to ☑).

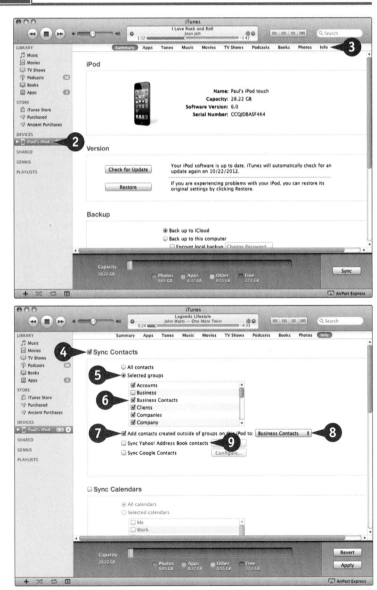

The Yahoo! Address Book dialog opens.

⑩ Type your Yahoo! ID.

⑪ Type your password.

⑫ Click **OK**.

The Yahoo! Address Book dialog closes.

**Note:** If you want to sync Google contacts, click **Sync Google Contacts** (☐ changes to ☑). Follow the procedure for setting up iTunes to access your Google account.

⑬ Click **Apply**.

iTunes syncs your chosen contacts with the iPod touch.

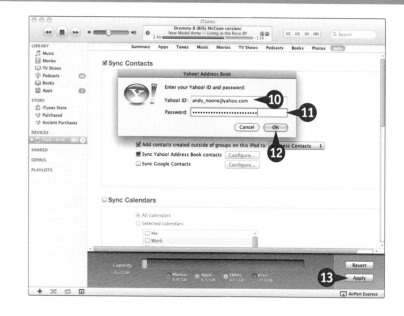

## TIP

**What happens if I change the same contact on my computer and my iPod touch?**

If you change contact information on your computer or your iPod touch, iTunes syncs the changes for you. But if you change the same information on both the computer and iPod touch between syncs, you create a sync conflict. When iTunes detects a sync conflict, it displays the Conflict Resolver dialog. Click **Review Now** (Ⓐ) to expand the Conflict Resolver dialog to see the details. You can then click the correct version of each contact record that has a conflict. Click **Done** to close the Conflict Resolver dialog.

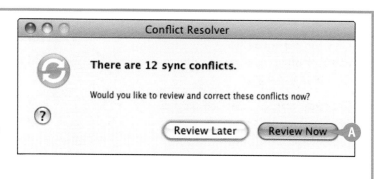

# Choose Which Calendars to Sync

To keep the same appointments and events on your iPod touch as on your PC or Mac, you can sync one or more calendars between your computer and the iPod touch. From the PC, you can sync the Outlook calendar; from the Mac, you can sync the calendars in the Calendar app.

If you have an iCloud account and use it to sync your calendars with your iPod touch, do not also synchronize them directly as described here. If you do, you may get duplicated calendar events on the iPod touch.

## Choose Which Calendars to Sync

**①** Connect the iPod touch to your PC or Mac.

iTunes launches or becomes active, and the iPod touch appears in the Devices list.

**②** Click your iPod touch.

The iPod touch's control screens appear, with the Summary screen at the front.

**③** Click **Info**.

The Info screen appears.

**④** Click **Sync Calendars** (☐ changes to ☑).

**Note:** In Windows, click **Sync calendars with** (☐ changes to ☑). You can then choose the program with which you want to sync — for example, Outlook.

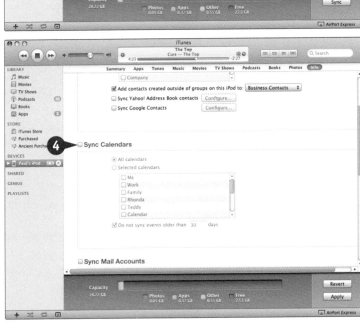

**⑤** To sync only some calendars, click **Selected calendars** ( ◯ changes to ◉ ).

The controls in the Selected Calendars box become available.

**⑥** Click the check box for each calendar you want to sync ( ☐ changes to ☑ ).

**⑦** To limit the number of days of calendar data, click **Do not sync events older than _N_ days** ( ☐ changes to ☑ ). Leave the default number, 30, or type a different number in the box.

**⑧** Click **Apply**.

iTunes syncs your chosen calendars to the iPod touch.

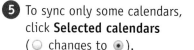

### Why should I choose not to sync events older than a certain number of days?

If your calendars contain many events, it is usually a good idea to use the Do Not Sync Events Older than _N_ Days option to limit the amount of data you sync between the iPod touch and your computer. You may want to change the number of days from the default, 30 — for example, set 90 days to sync around the last three months' worth of events. Limiting the number of days reduces the amount of data that iTunes must sync, which makes syncing faster. But if your calendars contain few events, or you need to carry details of your old events with you on the iPod touch, syncing all your calendar events is fine.

# Sync Mail Accounts with Your iPod touch

I f you need to be able to access your e-mail on your iPod touch, you can quickly sync one or more e-mail accounts from your PC or Mac. The iPod touch can access most types of e-mail accounts, including Gmail, Hotmail, Windows Mail, iCloud, Yahoo!, and Microsoft Exchange accounts.

## Sync Mail Accounts with Your iPod touch

**1** Connect the iPod touch to your PC or Mac.

iTunes launches or becomes active, and the iPod touch appears in the Devices list.

**2** Click your iPod touch.

The iPod touch's control screens appear, with the Summary screen at the front.

**3** Click **Info**.

The Info screen appears.

**4** Scroll down.

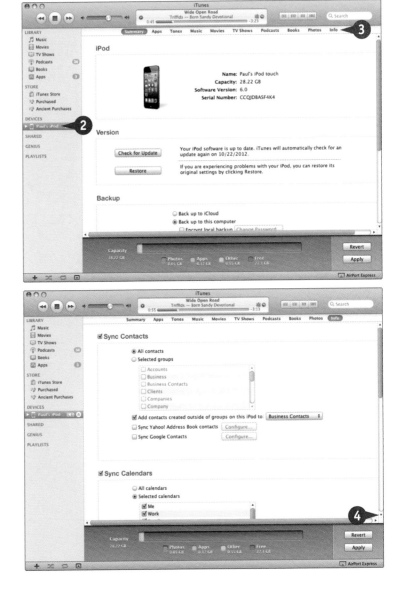

The Mail box appears with a list of accounts.

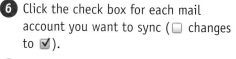 Click **Sync Mail Accounts** (☐ changes to ☑).

**Note:** In Windows, click **Sync selected mail accounts from** (☐ changes to ☑). Click the drop-down menu, and then click the program.

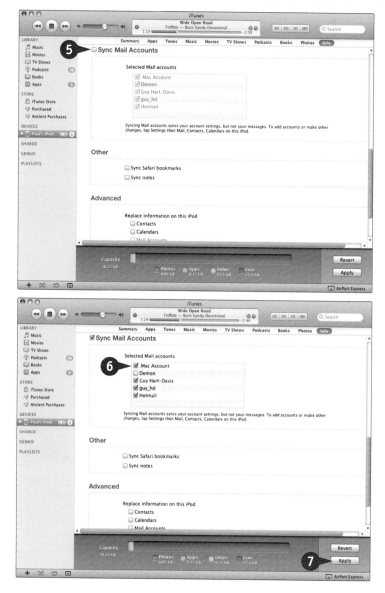

6️⃣ Click the check box for each mail account you want to sync (☐ changes to ☑).

7️⃣ Click **Apply**.

iTunes syncs the mail account details with the iPod touch.

## TIPS

**Can I add to the iPod touch an e-mail account that is not on my computer?**

Yes. You can set an e-mail account directly on the iPod touch. See Chapter 5 for instructions on how to set up an e-mail account.

**Do I need to sync with iTunes to get my e-mail on my iPod touch?**

No. You need only sync with iTunes to put the details of your e-mail accounts on the iPod touch. Once you have done that, you can get your e-mail directly on the iPod touch without involving your computer.

# Sync Bookmarks and Notes with Your iPod touch

To make browsing on the iPod touch faster and easier, you can sync your bookmarks from your computer's browser. Similarly, you can sync your notes from Outlook in Windows or from the Mail app on a Mac to the iPod touch's Notes app.

If you have an iCloud account and use it to sync your notes with your iPod touch, do not also synchronize them directly as described here. If you do, you may get duplicated notes on the iPod touch.

## Sync Bookmarks and Notes with Your iPod touch

**1** Connect the iPod touch to your PC or Mac.

iTunes launches or becomes active, and the iPod touch appears in the Devices list.

**2** Click your iPod touch.

The iPod touch's control screens appear, with the Summary screen at the front.

**3** Click **Info**.

The Info screen appears.

**4** Scroll down.

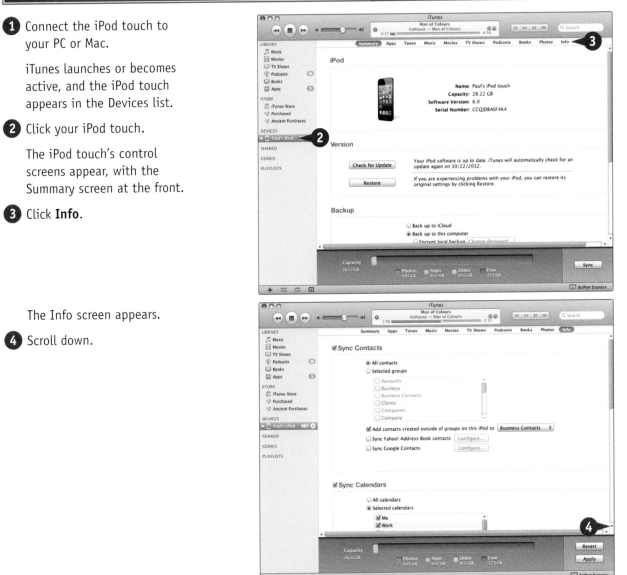

The Other box appears.

**5** Click **Sync Safari bookmarks**
(☐ changes to ☑).

**6** Click **Sync notes** (☐ changes
to ☑).

**7** Click **Apply**.

iTunes syncs the bookmarks
and notes with the iPod
touch.

**What do the options in the Advanced box on the Info screen do?**

The options in the Advanced box enable you to control which information iTunes overwrites on the iPod
touch when syncing.

Normally, when you first set up an iPod touch to sync items such as notes, bookmarks, or e-mail accounts,
you do not need to overwrite the data on the iPod touch.

But if the data on the iPod touch becomes corrupted, you can select the check boxes in the Advanced box
(☐ changes to ☑) to overwrite the iPod touch's data during the next sync. After overwriting the data,
iTunes clears these check boxes (☑ changes to ☐) so that it does not overwrite the data again.

**Advanced**

Replace information on this iPod

☐ Contacts
☐ Calendars
☑ Mail Accounts
☐ Bookmarks
☑ Notes

During the next sync only, iTunes will replace the selected information on this iPod with information from this
computer.

# Put Photos on Your iPod touch

As well as taking photos with the iPod touch's camera, you can load your existing photos on the iPod touch so that you can take them with you. You can then show the photos either on the iPod touch's screen or on a TV or an external monitor to which you connect the iPod touch.

iTunes enables you to copy all your photos to the iPod touch, but if you have many photos, they can take up all the free space on the device. So normally copying only selected photos to the iPod touch is best.

## Put Photos on Your iPod touch

1 Connect the iPod touch to your PC or Mac.

iTunes launches or becomes active, and the iPod touch appears in the Devices list.

2 Click your iPod touch.

The iPod touch's control screens appear, with the Summary screen at the front.

3 Click **Photos**.

The Photos screen appears.

4 Click **Sync Photos from** (☐ changes to ☑).

5 Open the pop-up menu and choose the source of the photos.

**Note:** In Windows, click **My Pictures** to sync with the My Pictures folder, or click **Choose Folder** and then select the folder. In OS X, click **iPhoto** to sync with your iPhoto library, or click **Choose Folder** and then select the folder.

**6** Click **Selected albums, Events, and Faces, and automatically include** (◯ changes to ⦿).

**7** Click the pop-up menu and then click an events option — for example, **the 3 most recent Events.**

**A** Click **Include videos** (☐ changes to ☑) if you want to include videos you have added to your iPhoto library. These are normally videos you have taken with your iPod touch or digital camera.

**8** Click the check box (☐ changes to ☑) for each album you want to include.

**9** Click the check box (☐ changes to ☑) for each event you want to add.

**10** Scroll down.

The Faces box appears.

**11** Click the check box (☐ changes to ☑) for each Face you want to sync.

**12** Click **Apply.**

iTunes syncs the photos to the iPod touch.

TIP

**How can I tell how much space the photos will take up on the iPod touch?**
Look at the readout at the bottom of the iTunes window. As you select different combinations of photos, albums, events, and faces, the readout changes to show how much space (**A**) your current choices will occupy.

# Put Books, Audiobooks, and PDF Files on Your iPod touch

Y ou can quickly install the free iBooks app on your iPod touch and use it to read books in formats such as the widely used ePub format. You can also open Portable Document Format (PDF) files in iBooks.

If you prefer to listen to your reading material, you can put audiobooks on the iPod touch instead, and then listen to them using the Music app.

## Put Books, Audiobooks, and PDF Files on Your iPod touch

**1** Connect the iPod touch to your PC or Mac.

iTunes launches or becomes active, and the iPod touch appears in the Devices list.

**2** Click your iPod touch.

The iPod touch's control screens appear, with the Summary screen at the front.

**3** Click **Books**.

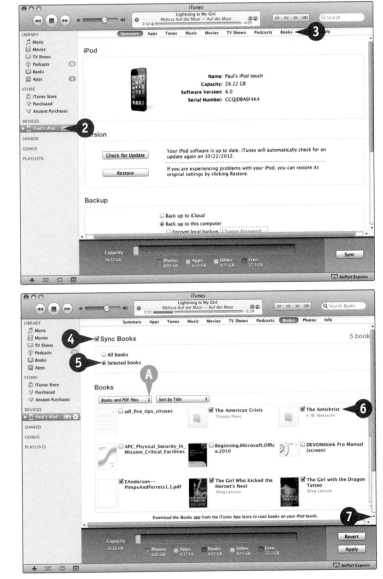

The Books screen appears.

**4** Click **Sync Books** (☐ changes to ☑).

The controls in the Sync Books box and the Books box become enabled.

**5** To sync only some books, click **Selected books** (○ changes to ●).

**6** Click the check box (☐ changes to ☑) for each book or PDF file you want to sync.

**A** If you have many books and PDF files, click the left pop-up menu and click **Only Books** or **Only PDF Files** to shorten the list.

**7** Scroll down.

The Audiobooks area appears.

⑧ Click **Sync Audiobooks** (☐ changes to ☑).

The controls in the Sync Audiobooks box become available.

⑨ To sync only some audiobooks, click **Selected audiobooks** (○ changes to ◉).

⑩ Click the check box (☐ changes to ☑) for each audiobook you want to include.

⑪ Click the check box (☑ changes to ☐) for any part you want to omit.

⑫ Scroll down.

The Include Audiobooks from Playlists box appears.

⑬ Click the check box (☐ changes to ☑) for each playlist of audiobooks to include.

⑭ Click **Apply**.

iTunes syncs the books and audiobooks.

**How do I make book files appear in the Audiobooks list?**

In iTunes, select the audio files you want to mark as audiobooks, and then click **File** and **Get Info**. If iTunes confirms that you want to edit information for multiple items, click **Yes**. In the Multiple Item Information dialog, click **Options** (Ⓐ). Click the **Media Kind** pop-up menu and then click **Audiobook** (Ⓑ). Click **OK**.

# Transfer Files to Your iPod touch Using iTunes File Sharing

When you need to transfer files to the iPod touch, you can use the File Sharing feature built into iTunes. This feature enables you to transfer files to the iPod touch's storage area devoted to a particular app. For example, when you need to use a file with the DocsToGo app on the iPod touch, you transfer to the DocsToGo area using File Sharing.

Only some apps can transfer files, and you must install an app capable of transferring files via File Sharing before you can use File Sharing as described in this task.

## Transfer Files to Your iPod touch Using iTunes File Sharing

**1** Connect the iPod touch to your PC or Mac.

iTunes launches or becomes active, and the iPod touch appears in the Devices list.

**2** Click your iPod touch.

The iPod touch's control screens appear, with the Summary screen at the front.

**3** Click **Apps**.

The Apps screen appears.

**4** Scroll down.

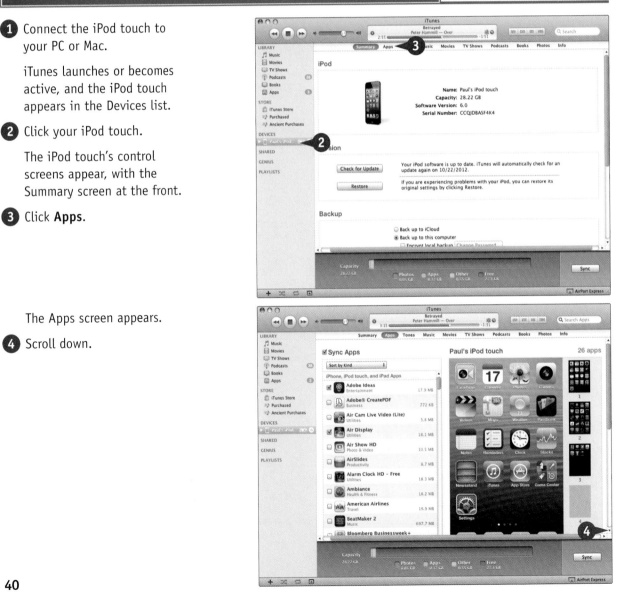

The File Sharing area appears.

**5** Click the app to which you want to add the file.

**6** Click **Add**.

The Open dialog appears.

**7** Click the file you want to copy to the iPod touch.

**Note:** You can copy multiple files at once by selecting them. For example, click the first file, and then Shift +click the last file to select a range of files.

**8** Click **Open**.

iTunes copies the file or files to the iPod touch.

---

**TIP**

**How do I copy a file from the iPod touch to my computer?**

**1** Open File Sharing as discussed in this task.

**2** In the Apps box, click the app that contains the file.

**3** In the Documents box, click the file.

**4** Click **Save to**. The Open dialog appears.

**5** Click the folder to save the file in.

**6** Click **Select Folder** in Windows or **Choose** on a Mac. iTunes copies the file.

# CHAPTER 3

# Personalizing Your iPod touch

To make your iPod touch work the way you prefer, you can configure its many settings. In this chapter, you learn how to control notifications, audio preferences, screen brightness, and other key aspects of the iPod touch's behavior.

# Find the Settings You Need

To configure the iPod touch, you work with its settings using the Settings app. This app contains settings for the iPod touch's system software, the apps the iPod touch includes, and third-party apps you have added. To reach the settings, you first display the Settings screen, and then display the category of settings you want to configure. Some apps provide access to settings through the apps themselves. So if you cannot find the settings for an app on the Settings screen, look within the app. In this task, you learn how to open the Settings screen and see the main categories of settings it contains.

## Find the Settings You Need

### Display the Settings Screen

**1** Press the Home button.

The Home screen appears.

**2** Tap **Settings**.

The Settings screen appears.

**3** Tap and drag up to scroll down the screen.

## Display a Settings Screen

**1** On the Settings screen, tap the button for the settings you want to display. For example, tap **Sounds** to display the Sounds screen.

**2** Tap **Settings** when you are ready to return to the Settings screen.

## Display the Settings for an App

**1** On the Settings screen, scroll down toward the bottom.

**2** Tap the button for the app whose settings you want to display. For example, tap **DEVONthink** to display the DEVONthink settings.

**3** Tap **Settings** when you are ready to return to the Settings screen.

**4** Press the Home button.

The Home screen appears again.

**TIP**

**Why do only some apps have a Settings entry?**

The Settings screen contains entries for only those apps that have settings you can configure. For example, the Nike + iPod app's settings include choosing your PowerSong, specifying your weight, and configuring the movement sensor. Other apps have no settings you can configure and so have no entry on the Settings screen.

# Choose Which Apps Can Give Notifications

Some iPod touch apps can notify you when you have received messages or when updates are available. You can choose which apps give which notifications, or prevent apps from showing notifications altogether. You can also choose the order in which the notifications appear in the Notifications Center and control which notifications appear on the lock screen.

iPod touch apps use three types of notifications. See the tip for details.

## Choose Which Apps Can Give Notifications

### Display the Notifications Screen

**1** Press the Home button.

The Home screen appears.

**A** A badge notification shows how many new items an app has.

**2** Tap **Settings**.

The Settings screen appears.

**3** Tap **Notifications**.

The Notifications screen appears.

### Choose How to Sort Apps That Give Notifications

**1** Tap **Manually** to use manual sorting for apps that give notifications. Tap **By Time** to have Notification Center sort the apps by the times of their notifications.

**2** Tap and drag up to scroll down the screen.

**B** The In Notification Center list appears, showing the apps currently set to appear in Notification Center.

## Choose Which Notifications Each App Can Give

**1** On the Notifications screen, tap the app's name.

The Notifications screen for the app appears.

**2** Move the **Notification Center** switch to On to have the app's notifications appear in Notification Center. Move the switch to Off if you do not want the notifications in Notification Center.

**3** Tap **Show**, tap the number of recent items to display, and then tap the app's name button to return.

**4** In the Alert Style box, tap **Alerts** to display alerts, **Banners** to display banners, or **None** to suppress alerts.

**5** Move the **Badge App Icon** switch to On to show badges or Off to hide them.

**6** Move the **Sounds** switch to On or Off.

**7** Move the **View in Lock Screen** switch to On or Off.

**8** Tap **Notifications** to return to the Notifications screen.

## TIP

**What are the three kinds of notifications?**

A *badge* (Ⓐ) is a red circle or rounded rectangle that appears on the app's icon on the Home screen and shows a white number indicating how many notifications there are. An *alert* (Ⓑ) is a text message that appears in front of the running app; you can also display an alert as a banner across the top of the screen. A *sound* notification plays a sound to get your attention.

# Choose Sounds Settings

To control how the iPod touch gives you audio feedback, choose settings on the Sounds screen. You can set the volume for the ringer and for alerts; choose your default ringtone and text tone; and choose whether to receive alerts for e-mail, calendar items, tweets, Facebook posts, and so on.

Playing lock sounds helps confirm that you have locked or unlocked the iPod touch as you intended. Playing keyboard clicks confirms each key press on the on-screen keyboard.

## Choose Sounds Settings

1 Press the Home button.

The Home screen appears.

2 Tap **Settings**.

The Settings screen appears.

3 Tap **Sounds**.

The Sounds screen appears.

4 Tap and drag the **Ringer and Alerts** slider to set the volume.

5 Tap the **Change with Buttons** switch and move it to On or Off as needed. When Change with Buttons is On, you can change the Ringer and Alerts volume by pressing the volume buttons on the side of the iPod touch.

6 Tap **Ringtone**.

The Ringtone screen appears.

7 Tap the ringtone you want to hear.

8 When you have chosen your ringtone, tap **Sounds**.

The Sounds screen appears again.

**9** Repeat steps **6** to **8** to set other tones: the text tone, new mail tone, and so on.

**10** Tap the **Lock Sounds** switch and move it to On or Off, as needed.

**11** Tap the **Keyboard Clicks** switch and move it to On or Off, as needed.

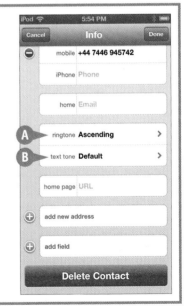

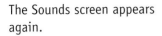

**How do I use different ringtones for different contacts?**
The ringtone and text tone you set in the Ringtone area of the Sounds screen are your standard tone for FaceTime calls and messaging calls. To set different tones for a contact, press the Home button, tap **Utilities**, and then tap **Contacts**. In the Contacts app, tap the contact, tap **Edit**, and then tap **ringtone** (Ⓐ). On the Ringtone screen, tap the ringtone, and then tap **Save**. To change the text tone, tap **text tone** (Ⓑ) and select the tone you want. Tap **Done** when you finish.

# Set Screen Brightness and Wallpaper Backgrounds

To make the screen easy to see, you can change its brightness. You can also have the iPod touch's Auto-Brightness feature automatically set the screen's brightness to a level suitable for the ambient brightness that the iPod touch's light sensor detects.

To make the screen attractive to your eye, you can choose which picture to use as the wallpaper that appears in the background. You can set different wallpaper for the lock screen — the screen you see when the iPod touch is locked — and for the Home screen.

## Set Screen Brightness and Wallpaper Backgrounds

**1** Press the Home button.

The Home screen appears.

**2** Tap **Settings**.

The Settings screen appears.

**3** Tap **Brightness & Wallpaper**.

The Brightness & Wallpaper screen appears.

**4** Tap the **Brightness** slider and drag it left or right to set brightness.

**5** Tap **Wallpaper**.

**Note:** The Wallpaper button is a single button, even though it looks like two buttons.

The Wallpaper screen appears, showing the list of picture categories.

 Tap **Wallpaper**.

 To choose a picture from a different picture category, tap that category. For example, tap **Camera Roll** to display pictures you have taken with the iPod touch's camera, saved from e-mail or multimedia messages, or web pages.

The Wallpaper category screen appears.

7 Tap the wallpaper you want.

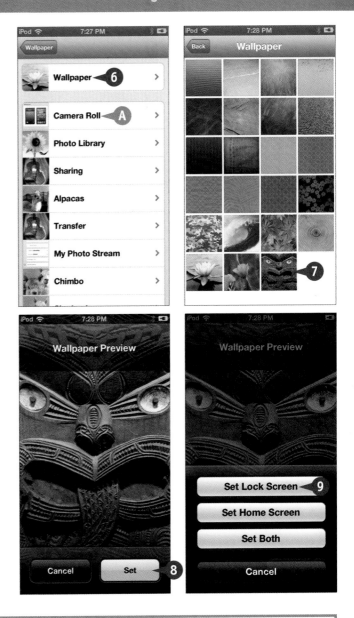

The Wallpaper Preview screen appears.

8 Tap **Set**.

9 Tap **Set Lock Screen**, **Set Home Screen**, or **Set Both**.

10 Tap **Back**.

11 Tap **Wallpaper**.

12 Tap **Settings**.

---

**TIP**

**How do I use only part of a picture as the wallpaper?**
The iPod touch wallpapers are the right size for the screen, so you do not need to resize them. But when you use a photo for the wallpaper, you usually need to choose which part of it to display. When you choose a photo as wallpaper, the iPod touch displays the screen for moving and scaling the photo. Pinch in or out to zoom the photo out or in, and tap and drag to move the picture around. When you have chosen the part you want, tap **Set**.

# Choose Privacy and Location Settings

Your iPod touch contains a huge amount of information about you, the people you communicate with, what you do, and where you go. To keep this information safe, you need to choose suitable privacy and location settings.

Privacy settings enable you to control which apps may access your contacts, calendars, reminders, and photos. You can also choose which apps can use your iPod touch's Location Services, which track the iPod touch's location by finding known wireless networks nearby and triangulating its position.

## Choose Privacy and Location Settings

**1** Press the Home button.

The Home screen appears.

**2** Tap **Settings**.

The Settings screen appears.

**3** Tap **Privacy**.

The Privacy screen appears.

**4** Tap **Location Services**.

The Location Services screen appears.

**5** If you need to turn location services off completely, tap the **Location Services** switch and move it to Off.

**6** Tap the switch for an app, and move it to On or Off, as needed. For example, tap the **Camera** switch and move it to On.

**7** Tap **Find My iPod**.

The Find My iPod screen appears.

**8** Tap the **Find My iPod** switch and move it to On if you want to be able to locate your iPod touch should it go missing.

**9** Tap the **Status Bar Icon** switch and move it to On if you want to see an arrow in the status bar when the iPod touch is being tracked.

**10** Tap **Location Services**.

**11** Scroll down to the bottom of the Location Services screen and tap **System Services**.

The System Services screen appears.

**12** Tap the switch for a system service, and move it to On or Off, as needed.

**13** Tap **Location Services**.

**14** On the Location Services screen, tap **Privacy**.

**15** On the Privacy screen, tap **Contacts**.

**16** Set the switches to choose which apps can access your contacts.

**17** Tap **Privacy**, and then repeat steps **15** and **16** for Calendars, Reminders, and Photos.

**TIP**

**Why do some apps need to use location services?**

Some apps and system services need to use location services to determine where you are. For example, the Maps app needs to use location services so that it can display your location, and the Compass service needs to learn your position in order to display accurate compass information.

If you allow the Camera app to use location services, it stores location data in your photos. You can then sort the photos by location in applications such as iPhoto on OS X. Other apps use location services to provide context-specific information, such as information about nearby restaurants. It is a good idea to review which apps are using location services and to turn off any that do not have a compelling reason for doing so.

# Configure Spotlight Search to Find What You Need

Your iPod touch can put a huge amount of data in the palm of your hand, and you may often need to search to find what you need.

To make your search results more accurate and helpful, you can configure your iPod touch's Spotlight Search feature. You can turn off searching for items you do not want to see in your search results, and you can change the order in which Spotlight displays the items it finds.

## Configure Spotlight Search to Find What You Need

**1** Press the Home button.

The Home screen appears.

**2** Tap **Settings**.

The Settings screen appears.

**3** Tap **General**.

The General screen appears.

**4** Tap **Spotlight Search**.

The Spotlight Search screen appears.

**5** Tap to remove the check mark from each item you do not want to search.

**6** Tap a movement handle and drag an item up or down the search order.

**Note:** Spotlight displays the search results in descending order, starting with the first item on the list.

**7** Tap **General** to go back to the General screen.

**8** Tap **Settings** to go back to the Settings screen.

---

**TIP**

**Which items should I make Spotlight search?**
This depends on what you need to be able to search for. For example, if you do not need to search for music, videos, or podcasts, remove the check marks for the Music, Podcasts, and Videos item on the Spotlight Search screen to exclude them from Spotlight searches. For normal use, you may want to leave all the check marks in place but move the items most important to you to the top of the Spotlight Search list.

# Choose Locking and Sleep Settings

To avoid unintentional taps on the screen, your iPod touch automatically locks itself after a period of inactivity. After locking itself, your iPod touch turns off its screen and goes to sleep to save battery power.

You can choose how long your iPod touch waits before locking itself. Setting your iPod touch to lock quickly helps preserve battery power, but you may prefer to leave your iPod touch on longer so that you can continue work. You can then lock your iPod touch manually.

## Choose Locking and Sleep Settings

**1** Press the Home button.

The Home screen appears.

**2** Tap **Settings**.

The Settings screen appears.

**3** Tap **General**.

The General screen appears.

**4** Tap **Auto-Lock**.

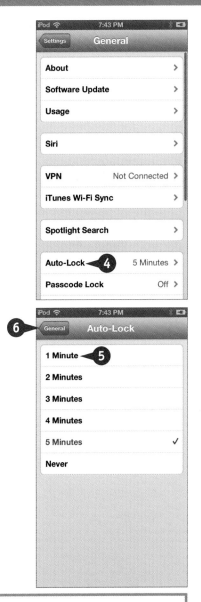

The Auto-Lock screen appears.

**5** Tap the interval — for example, **1 Minute**.

**6** Tap **General**.

The General screen appears.

**How do I put the iPod touch to sleep manually?**
You can put the iPod touch to sleep at any point by pressing the Power/Sleep button for a moment.

Putting the iPod touch to sleep as soon as you stop using it helps to prolong battery life. If you apply a passcode, as discussed later in this chapter, putting the iPod touch to sleep also starts protecting your data sooner.

**When should I use the Never setting for Auto-Lock?**
Choose the Never setting for Auto-Lock if you need to make sure the iPod touch never goes to sleep. For example, if you are playing music with the lyrics displayed, turning off auto-locking like this may be helpful.

# Set Up and Use Do Not Disturb Mode

When you do not want your iPod touch to disturb you, turn on its Do Not Disturb mode. You can configure Do Not Disturb mode to turn on and off automatically at set times each day. For example, you can set Do Not Disturb mode to turn on at 10 PM and off at 7 AM. You can turn Do Not Disturb mode on and off manually, as needed.

Optionally, you can allow particular groups of contacts to bypass Do Not Disturb mode so they can contact you even when Do Not Disturb is on.

## Set Up and Use Do Not Disturb Mode

### Configure Do Not Disturb Mode

**1** Press the Home button.

The Home screen appears.

**2** Tap **Settings**.

The Settings screen appears.

**3** Tap **Notifications**.

The Notifications screen appears.

**4** Tap **Do Not Disturb**.

The Do Not Disturb screen appears.

**5** If you want to schedule your quiet hours, tap the **Scheduled** switch and move it to the On position.

The From, To button appears.

**6** Tap **From, To**.

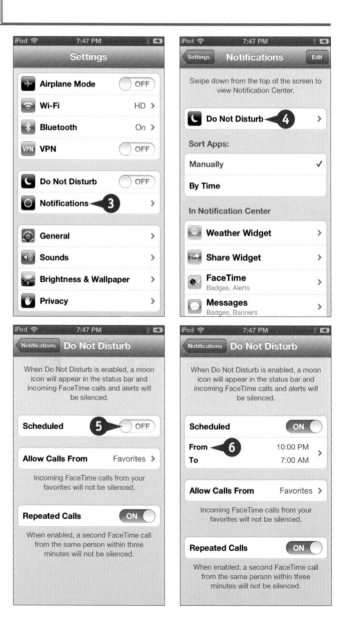

**7** On the Quiet Hours screen, tap **From**.

**8** Use the spin wheels to set the From time.

**9** Tap **To**.

**10** Set the To time.

**11** Tap **Do Not Disturb**.

**12** Tap **Allow Calls From**.

**13** On the Allow Calls From screen, tap the group you will allow to contact you during your quiet hours.

**14** Tap **Do Not Disturb**.

**15** Tap the **Repeated Calls** switch and set it to On or Off, as needed. Setting Repeated Calls to On allows a second call from the same number within three minutes to breach your Do Not Disturb zone.

**16** Tap **Notifications**.

## Turn Do Not Disturb Mode On or Off Manually

**1** Press the Home button.

**2** On the Home screen, tap **Settings**.

**3** On the Settings screen, tap the **Do Not Disturb** switch and move it to the On position or the Off position, as needed.

---

**TIP**

**How can I tell whether Do Not Disturb is on?**
When Do Not Disturb is on, a crescent moon symbol (Ⓐ) appears in the status bar to the left of the time.

# Secure Your iPod touch with a Passcode Lock

To prevent anyone who picks up your iPod touch from accessing your data, you can lock the iPod touch with a passcode. This is a code that takes effect when you lock your iPod touch or it locks itself. When you unlock the iPod touch, you must provide the passcode.

For added security, you can set the iPod touch to automatically erase its data after ten failed attempts to enter the passcode. You can also choose between a standard, four-digit password and a longer password in which you can use numbers, letters, and other characters.

## Secure Your iPod touch with a Passcode Lock

**1** Press the Home button.

The Home screen appears.

**2** Tap **Settings**.

The Settings screen appears.

**3** Tap **General**.

The General screen appears.

**4** Tap **Passcode Lock**.

The Passcode Lock screen appears.

**5** To follow this example, make sure the **Simple Passcode** switch is On. If not, tap and move it to On.

**6** Tap **Turn Passcode On**.

The Set Passcode screen appears.

**Note:** The iPod touch shows dots instead of your passcode digits in case someone is watching.

**7** Type your passcode.

The iPod touch displays the Set Passcode screen again, this time with the message "Re-enter your passcode."

**8** Type the passcode again.

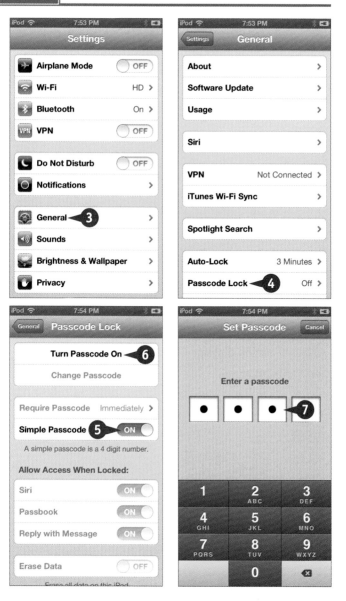

The Passcode Lock screen appears.

**9** Tap **Require Passcode**.

The Require Passcode screen appears.

**10** Tap the button for the length of time you want — for example, **After 1 minute** or **Immediately**.

**11** Tap **Passcode Lock**.

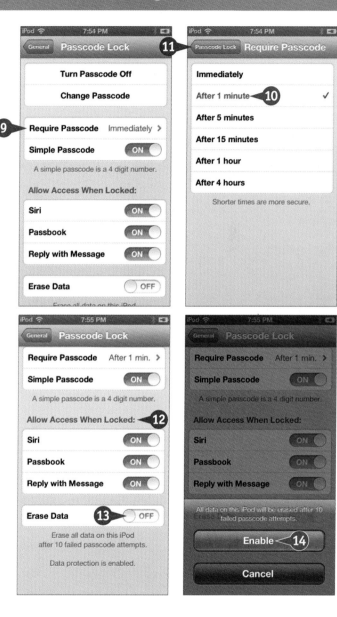

The Passcode Lock screen appears.

**12** In the Allow Access When Locked box, set the **Siri** switch, the **Passbook** switch, and the **Reply with Message** switch to Off or On, as needed.

**13** If you want the iPod touch to erase all its data after ten failed passcode attempts, tap the **Erase Data** switch and move it to On.

The iPod touch displays a confirmation dialog.

**14** Tap **Enable**.

## TIPS

**How can I make my passcode even more secure?**
If you feel a four-digit passcode is not secure enough, tap the **Simple Passcode** switch on the Passcode Lock screen and move it to Off. When you tap **Turn Passcode On**, the Set Passcode screen lets you set a passcode of any length.

**What Require Passcode setting should I choose?**
Choose **Immediately** for greatest security. Choose **After 1 minute** for good security but more convenience.

# Configure Restrictions and Parental Controls

Like any other computer than can access the Internet, the iPod touch can reach vast amounts of content not suitable for children or business contexts.

You can restrict the iPod touch from accessing particular kinds of content. You can use the restrictions to implement parental controls — for example, preventing the iPod touch's user from buying content in apps or watching adult-rated movies.

## Configure Restrictions and Parental Controls

**1** Press the Home button.

The Home screen appears.

**2** Tap **Settings**.

The Settings screen appears.

**3** Tap **General**.

The General screen appears.

**4** Scroll down, and then tap **Restrictions**.

The Restrictions screen appears.

**5** Tap **Enable Restrictions**.

The Set Passcode screen appears.

**Note:** The passcode you set to protect restrictions is different from the passcode you use to lock the iPod touch. Do not use the same code.

**6** Type the passcode.

**Note:** The iPod touch shows dots instead of your passcode digits in case someone is watching.

The iPod touch displays the Set Passcode screen again, this time with the message "Re-enter your Restrictions Passcode."

**7** Type the passcode again.

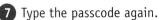

The Restrictions screen appears with the controls in the Allow box now available.

**8** In the Allow box, move each switch to On or Off, as needed.

**9** Scroll down to the Allowed Content box.

**10** If you need to change the country used for rating content, tap **Ratings For**. On the Ratings For screen, tap the country, and then tap **Restrictions**.

**11** Choose settings for Music & Podcasts, Movies, TV Shows, and Apps. For example, tap **Movies**.

**12** On the Movies screen, tap the highest rating you will permit.

**13** Tap **Restrictions**.

**14** Move the **In-App Purchases** switch to Off to prevent the user buying items from within apps.

**15** Choose other settings in the Privacy box.

**16** Choose settings for Accounts, Find My Friends, and Volume Limit.

**17** Move the **Multiplayer Games** switch and the **Adding Friends** switch to On or Off, as needed.

**TIPS**

**What are in-app purchases?**
In-app purchases are items that you can buy from within apps without needing to use the App Store app. These are a popular and easy way for developers to sell extra features for apps, especially low-cost apps or free apps. They are also an easy way for the iPod touch's user to spend money.

**What do the Privacy settings in Restrictions do?**
The Privacy settings in Restrictions enable you to control which apps can access the iPod touch's location information, contacts, calendars, reminders, and photos.

To keep yourself on time and your data accurate, you need to make sure the iPod touch is using the correct date and time.

To make dates, times, and other data appear in the formats you prefer, you may need to change the iPod touch's International settings.

## Choose Date, Time, and International Settings

### Choose Date and Time Settings

**1** Press the Home button.

The Home screen appears.

**2** Tap **Settings**.

The Settings screen appears.

**3** Tap **General**.

The General screen appears.

**4** Scroll down to the bottom.

**5** Tap **Date & Time**.

The Date & Time screen appears.

**6** Tap the **24-Hour Time** switch and move it to On if you want to use 24-hour times.

**7** To set the date and time manually, tap the **Set Automatically** switch and move it to Off.

**8** Tap **Set Date & Time**.

Another Date & Time screen appears.

**9** Set the date and time.

**10** Tap **Date & Time**.

**11** Tap **General**.

The General screen appears.

## Choose International Settings

**1** From the General screen, tap **International**.

The International screen appears.

**2** Tap **Region Format**.

The Region Format screen appears.

**3** Tap the region you want, placing a check mark next to it.

**4** Tap **International**.

The International screen appears.

**Note:** From the International screen, you can also change the language used for the iPod touch's user interface and the language used for voice control.

---

**TIP**

**How does the iPod touch set the date and time automatically?**

The iPod touch sets the date and time automatically by using time servers, computers on the Internet that provide date and time information to computers that request them. The iPod touch automatically determines its geographical location so that it can request the right time zone from the time server.

# Set Up Your Facebook and Twitter Accounts

Your iPod touch has built-in support for posting updates to your Facebook and Twitter accounts. For example, you can quickly create a post or a tweet from the Notifications screen, or you can share a photo from the Photos app or the Camera app.

Before you can use Facebook or Twitter, you must enter the details of your account as described in this task.

## Set Up Your Facebook and Twitter Accounts

**1** Press the Home button.

**Note:** If you try to post an update to Facebook or Twitter before you set up your account, your iPod touch automatically prompts you for the account details.

The Home screen appears.

**2** Tap **Settings**.

The Settings screen appears.

**3** Scroll down until you see the box containing the Twitter button and the Facebook button.

**4** Tap **Twitter**.

The Twitter screen appears.

**5** Type your username.

**Note:** If you do not have a Twitter account, tap **Create New Account** and follow the resulting screens to create an account.

**6** Type your password.

**7** Tap **Sign In**.

Twitter verifies your username and password, and then sets up your account on the iPod touch.

**8** Tap **Settings**.

The Settings screen appears.

**9** Tap **Facebook**.

10 On the Facebook screen, type your username.

11 Type your password.

12 Tap **Sign In**.

13 On the next Facebook screen, tap **Sign In**.

Facebook verifies your username and password.

**Note:** If your iPod touch prompts you to install the Facebook app, tap **Install.** The Settings button appears on the Facebook screen only when you have installed the Facebook app.

14 Back on the Facebook screen, tap **Settings**.

15 On the Settings screen, set the **Vibrate** switch and **Play Sound** switch to control which chat and message alerts you get.

**Note:** The iPod touch does not have a vibration unit, so you will not get vibration even if you set the Vibrate switch to On.

16 Set the **Record HD Video** switch to On or Off, as needed.

17 Tap **Facebook**.

18 Tap **Settings**.

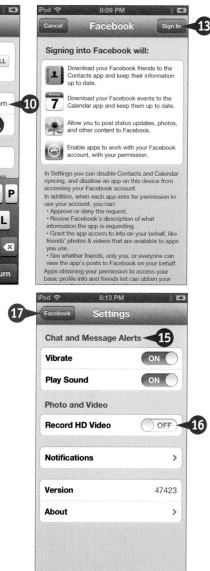

**How do I start a Facebook post or a tweet?**
You can start a Facebook post or a Twitter tweet in various ways. Perhaps the easiest way is to open the Notifications screen and then tap the **Tap to Tweet** button for Twitter or the **Tap to Post** button for Facebook.

# CHAPTER 4

# Working with Siri and Dictation

To enable you to give voice commands and dictate text, your iPod touch includes the powerful personal assistant called Siri.

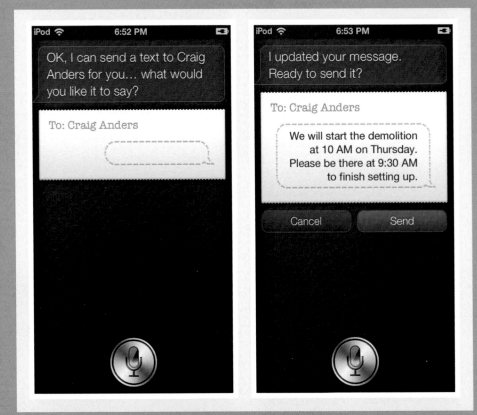

# Give Commands with Siri

Often, speaking is easier than using your iPod touch's touch screen — especially when you are out and about or on the move. The iPod touch's powerful Siri feature enables you to take essential actions by using your voice to tell your iPod touch what you want. Siri requires an Internet connection, because the speech recognition runs on servers in Apple's data center.

You can use Siri either with the iPod touch's built-in microphone or with the microphone on the headset. Unless you are in a quiet environment, or you hold your iPod touch close to your face, the headset microphone gives much better results than the built-in microphone.

## Open Siri

From the Home screen or any app, press the Home button or the headset clicker button for several seconds. The Siri screen appears. A tone indicates that Siri is ready to take your commands.

## Send an E-Mail Message

Say "E-mail" and the contact's name, followed by the message. Siri creates an e-mail message to the contact and enters the text. Review the message, and then tap **Send** to send it.

## Send a Text Message

Say "Tell" and the contact's name. When Siri responds, say the message you want to send. For example, say "Tell Chris Smith" and then "I'm stuck in traffic but I'll be there in an hour." Siri creates a text message to the contact, enters the text, and sends the message.

You can also say "tell" and the contact's name followed immediately by the message. For example, "Tell Bill Sykes the package will arrive at 10 a.m."

## Set a Reminder for Yourself

Say "Remind me" and the details of what you want Siri to remind you of. For example, say "Remind me to take my iPad to Acme Industries tomorrow morning." Siri listens to what you say and creates a reminder. Check what Siri has written, and then tap **Confirm** if it is correct.

## Set an Alarm

Say "Set an alarm for 5 a.m." and check the alarm that Siri displays.

## Set Up a Meeting

Say "Meet with" and the contact's name, followed by brief details of the appointment. For example, say "Meet with Don Williamson for lunch at noon on Friday." Siri listens, sends a meeting invitation to the contact if it finds an e-mail address, and adds the meeting to your calendar.

# Dictate Text Using Siri

**O**ne of Siri's strongest features is the capability to transcribe your speech quickly and accurately into correctly spelled and punctuated text. Using your iPod touch, you can dictate into any app that supports the keyboard, so you can dictate e-mail messages, notes, documents, and more. To dictate, simply tap the microphone icon (🎤), speak after Siri beeps, and then tap **Done**.

To get the most out of dictation, it is helpful to know the standard terms for dictating punctuation, capitalization, symbols, layout, and formatting.

## Insert Punctuation

To insert punctuation, use standard terms: "comma," "period" (or "full stop"), "semicolon," "colon," "exclamation point" (or "exclamation mark"), "question mark," "hyphen," "dash" (for a short dash, –), or "em dash" (for a long dash, —).

You can also say "asterisk" (*), "ampersand" (&), "open parenthesis" and "close parenthesis," "open bracket" and "close bracket," and "underscore" (_).

buy eggs comma bread comma and cheese semicolon and maybe some milk period nothing else exclamation point

iPod 7:09 PM

❝ Buy eggs, bread, and cheese; and maybe some milk. Nothing else! ❞

## Insert Standard Symbols

To insert symbols, use these terms: "at sign" (@), "percent sign" (%), "greater-than sign" (>) and "less-than sign" (<), "forward slash" (/) and "backslash" (\), "registered sign" (®), and "copyright sign" (©).

fifty-eight percent sign forward slash two greater-than sign ninety-seven percent sign forward slash three

iPod 7:09 PM

What can I help you with?

❝ 58%/2 > 97%/3 ❞

OK, Gary, here you go:

Input interpretation
$$\frac{58\%}{2} > \frac{97\%}{3}$$
Result
False
WolframAlpha

## Insert Currency Symbols

To insert currency symbols, say the currency name and "sign." For example, say "dollar sign" to insert $, "cent sign" to insert ¢, "euro sign" to insert €, "pound sterling sign" to insert £, and "yen sign" to insert ¥.

dollar sign nine equals pound sterling sign six

iPod 7:09 PM

❝ $9 equals £6 ❞

This might answer your question:

Input interpretation
$9 (US dollars) = £6 (British pounds)
Result
False
WolframAlpha

## Control Layout

You can control layout by creating new lines and new paragraphs as needed. A new paragraph enters two blank lines, creating a blank line between paragraphs.

To create a new line, say "new line." To create a new paragraph, say "new paragraph."

> dear Anna comma new paragraph thank you for the parrot period new paragraph it's the most amazing gift I've ever had period

## Control Capitalization

You can apply capitalization to the first letter of a word or to a whole word. You can also switch capitalization off temporarily to force lowercase:

- Say "cap" to capitalize the first letter of the next word.

- Say "caps on" to capitalize all the words until you say "caps off."

- Say "no caps" to prevent automatic capitalization of the next word — for example, "no caps Monday" produces "monday" instead of "Monday."

- Say "no caps on" to force lowercase of all words until you say "no caps off."

> give the cap head cap dining cap table a no caps French polish period

## Insert Quotes and Emoticons

To insert double quotes, say "open quotes" and "close quotes." To insert single quotes, say "open single quotes" and "close single quotes."

To enter standard emoticons, say "smiley face," "frown face," and "wink face."

> she said open quotes I want to go to Paris next summer exclamation point close quotes

# Gather and Share Information with Siri

You can use Siri to research a wide variety of information online — everything from sports and movies to restaurants worth visiting or worth avoiding. You can also use Siri to perform hands-free calculations.

When you need to share information quickly and easily, you can turn to Siri. By giving the right commands, you can quickly change your Facebook status or post on your wall. Similarly, you can send tweets on your Twitter account.

### Find Information about Sports

Launch Siri and ask a question about sports. For example:

- "Siri, when's the next White Sox game?"

- "Did the Lakers win their last game?"

- "When's the end of the NBA season?"

### Find Information about Movies

Launch Siri and ask a question about movies. For example:

- "Siri, where is the movie *Hotel Transylvania* playing in Chicago?"

- "What's the name of Blake Lively's latest movie?"

- "Who's the star of *The Amazing Spider-Man*?"

### Find a Restaurant

Launch Siri, and then tell Siri what type of restaurant you want. For example:

- "Where's the best Chinese food in Oakland?"

- "Where can I get sushi in Albuquerque?"

- "Is there a brew-pub in Minneapolis?"

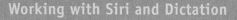
## Address a Query to the Wolfram Alpha Computational Knowledge Engine

Launch Siri, and then say "Wolfram" and your question. For example, say "Wolfram, what is the cube of 27?"

## Update Your Facebook Status or Post a Comment on Your Wall

Launch Siri and give the appropriate command:

- "Update my Facebook status," and then give details when Siri prompts you.

- "Post on my Facebook wall," and then dictate the post when Siri prompts you.

## Send a Tweet

Launch Siri, and then say "Tweet" and the text of the tweet. Tap **Add Location** if you want to add your current location to the tweet.

# Configure Siri to Work Your Way

To get the most out of Siri, spend a few minutes configuring Siri. You can set the language Siri uses and choose when Siri should give you voice feedback.

Most importantly, you can tell Siri which contact record contains your information, so that Siri knows your name, address, phone numbers, e-mail address, and other essential information.

## Configure Siri to Work Your Way

1 Press the Home button.

The Home screen appears.

2 Tap **Settings**.

The Settings screen appears.

3 Tap **General**.

The General screen appears.

4 Tap **Siri**.

The Siri screen appears.

5 Make sure the **Siri** switch is in the On position if you want to use Siri.

6 Tap **Language**.

The Language screen appears.

⑦ Tap the language you want to use, placing a check mark next to it.

⑧ Tap **Siri**.

The Siri screen appears.

⑨ Tap **Voice Feedback**.

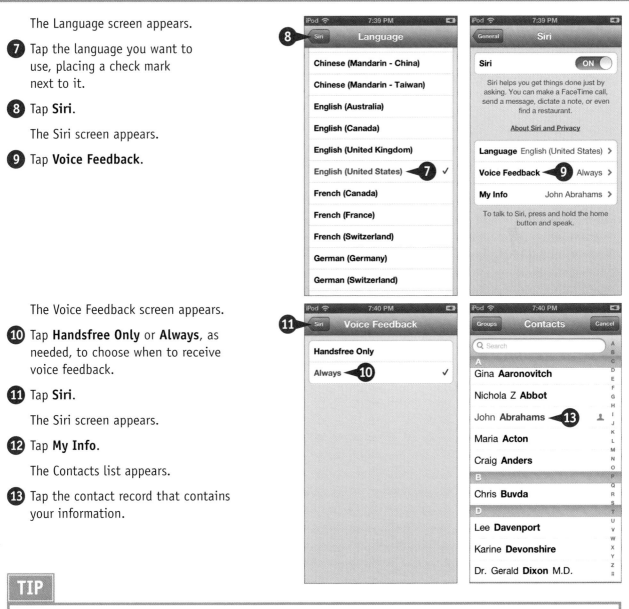

The Voice Feedback screen appears.

⑩ Tap **Handsfree Only** or **Always**, as needed, to choose when to receive voice feedback.

⑪ Tap **Siri**.

The Siri screen appears.

⑫ Tap **My Info**.

The Contacts list appears.

⑬ Tap the contact record that contains your information.

---

**TIP**

**Does Apple store the details of what I ask Siri?**
Yes, but not in a way that will come back to haunt you. When you use Siri, your iPod touch passes your input to servers in Apple's data center in North Carolina, U.S.A, for processing. The servers analyze your request and tell Siri how to respond to it. Apple's data center stores the details of your request and may analyze them to determine what people use Siri for and work out ways of making Siri more effective. Apple does not associate your Siri data with other data Apple holds about you — for example, the identity and credit card data you used to pay for iTunes Match.

# CHAPTER 5

# Setting Up Mail and Calendar

In this chapter, you learn how to add your e-mail accounts to the Mail app and choose options for your calendars and notes. You also learn how to send instant messages and chat face-to-face with FaceTime.

The easiest way to set up an e-mail account on your iPod touch is to synchronize the details from your PC or Mac, as discussed in Chapter 2. But if the e-mail account is not set up on the computer with which you synchronize the iPod touch, you can set the account up directly on the iPod touch as explained in this task.

To set up an e-mail account, you need to know the e-mail address and password, as well as the e-mail provider. You may also need to know the addresses of the mail servers the account uses. For Microsoft Exchange, you must know the domain name as well.

## Set Up Your Mail Accounts

**1** Press the Home button.

The Home screen appears.

**2** Tap **Settings**.

The Settings screen appears.

**Note:** If you have not yet set up an e-mail account on the iPod touch, you can also open the Add Account screen by tapping **Mail** on the iPod touch's Home screen.

**3** Tap and drag up to scroll down until the third group of buttons appears.

**4** Tap **Mail, Contacts, Calendars**.

The Mail, Contacts, Calendars screen appears.

**5** Tap **Add Account**.

**Note:** This example uses a Gmail account. Setting up a Yahoo! account or an AOL account uses the same fields of information. For an iCloud account, you enter only the e-mail address and password. For details on setting up an iCloud account, see the tip.

**6** On the Add Account screen, tap the kind of account you want to set up.

The screen for setting up that type of account appears.

**7** Tap **Name** and type your name as you want it to appear in messages you send.

**8** Tap **Email** and type the e-mail address.

**9** Tap **Password** and type the password.

**10** Tap **Description** and type a descriptive name.

**11** Tap **Next**.

**12** On the configuration screen for the account, make sure the **Mail** switch is set to On.

**13** Tap the **Calendars** switch and move it to On or Off.

**14** Tap the **Notes** switch and move it to On or Off.

**15** Tap **Save**.

Ⓐ The account appears on the Mail, Contacts, Calendars screen.

**TIP**

**How do I change the name for an iCloud account?**
When you set up an iCloud account, the iCloud screen prompts you for only your Apple ID (which is your e-mail address) and password. The account appears under the name iCloud in the Accounts list on the Mail, Contacts, Calendars screen. To change the name, press the Home button and then tap **Settings**. Scroll down to display the third group of buttons and tap **Mail, Contacts, Calendars**. Tap the iCloud account and then tap **Account**. Tap **Description** and type the name to identify the account. Tap **Done** and then tap **Mail, Contacts, Calendars**.

# Control How the iPod touch Displays Your E-Mail

To make your iPod touch's Mail app easy to use, you can choose settings that suit the way you work.

You can choose how many messages to show in each mailbox and how many lines to include in the preview. To make messages easy to read, you can change the minimum font size. You can also choose whether to load remote images in messages.

## Control How the iPod touch Displays Your E-Mail

**1** Press the Home button.

The Home screen appears.

**2** Tap **Settings**.

The Settings screen appears.

**3** Tap and drag up to scroll down until the third group of buttons appears.

**4** Tap **Mail, Contacts, Calendars**.

The Mail, Contacts, Calendars screen appears.

**5** If necessary, tap and drag up to scroll down a little way.

The Mail options appear.

⑥ Tap **Show**.

⑦ On the Show screen, tap the number of messages you want.

⑧ Tap **Mail, Contacts, Calendars**.

⑨ On the Mail, Contacts, Calendars screen, tap **Preview**.

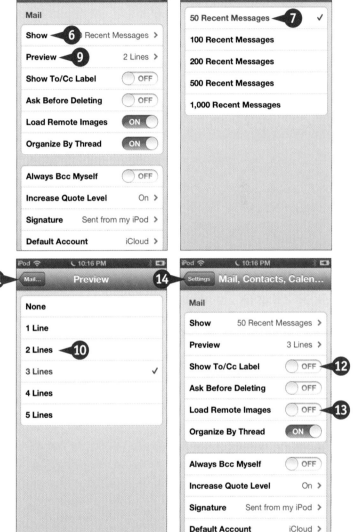

⑩ On the Preview screen, tap the number of lines you want to see in previews.

⑪ Tap **Mail, Contacts, Calendars**.

⑫ On the Mail, Contacts, Calendars screen, tap the **Show To/Cc Label** switch and move it to On or Off.

⑬ Tap the **Load Remote Images** switch and move it to On or Off.

**Note:** Loading a remote image enables the sender to learn that you have opened the message. When Mail requests the remote image, the server that provides the image can log the date and time and tie it to the message sent to you. The server can also learn your Internet connection's IP address and determine your approximate location.

⑭ Tap **Settings**.

**TIP**

**What is the Always Bcc Myself setting useful for?**

Most e-mail services automatically put a copy of each message you send or forward into a folder with a name such as Sent, so that you can easily review the messages you have sent. If your e-mail service does not use a Sent folder, move the Always Bcc Myself switch to On to send a bcc copy of each message to yourself. You can then file these messages in a folder of your choosing — for example, a folder named Sent — to keep a record of your sent messages.

# Organize Your E-Mail Messages by Thread

The Mail app gives you two ways to view e-mail messages. You can view the messages as a simple list, or you can view them with related messages organized into *threads*, which are sometimes called *conversations*.

Having Mail display your messages as threads can help you navigate your Inbox quickly and find related messages easily. You may find threading useful if you tend to have long e-mail conversations, because threading reduces the number of messages you see at once.

## Organize Your E-Mail Messages by Thread

### Set Mail to Organize Your Messages by Thread

1 Press the Home button.

The Home screen appears.

2 Tap **Settings**.

The Settings screen appears.

3 Tap and drag up to scroll down until the third group of buttons appears.

4 Tap **Mail, Contacts, Calendars**.

The Mail, Contacts, Calendars screen appears.

5 Tap and drag up to scroll down a little way.

The Mail options appear.

6 Tap the **Organize By Thread** switch and move it to the On position.

## Read Messages Organized into Threads

**1** Press the Home button.

The Home screen appears.

**2** Tap **Mail**.

The Mailboxes screen appears.

**3** Tap the mailbox.

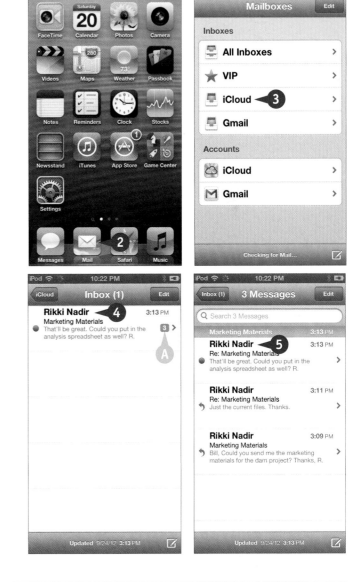

The Inbox for the account appears.

**A** A number on the right indicates a threaded message.

**4** Tap the threaded message.

A screen showing the threaded message appears.

**5** Tap the message you want to display.

**Is there a quick way to enter my name and information at the end of a message?**

Yes. You can create one or more e-mail signatures, which are sections of predefined text that Mail can insert at the end of messages. From the Home screen, tap **Settings**, and then tap **Mail, Contacts, Calendars**. Scroll down and tap **Signature** to display the Signature screen. Tap **All Accounts** to use the same signature for each account, or tap **Per Account** to use a different signature for each account. Then type the text to use.

# Set Your Default E-Mail Account

I f you set up two or more e-mail accounts on your iPod touch, make sure that you set the right e-mail account to be the default account. The default account is the one from which the Mail app sends messages unless you choose another account, so choosing the appropriate account is important.

## Set Your Default E-Mail Account

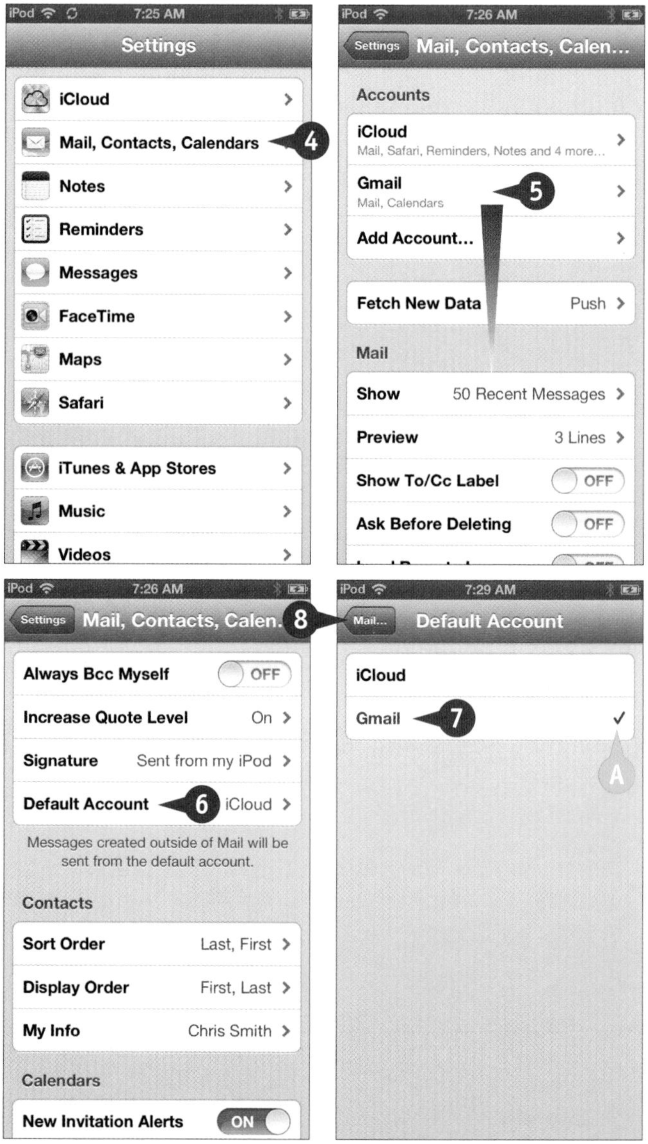

**1** Press the Home button.

The Home screen appears.

**2** Tap **Settings**.

The Settings screen appears.

**3** Tap and drag up to scroll down until the fourth group of buttons appears.

**4** Tap **Mail, Contacts, Calendars**.

The Mail, Contacts, Calendars screen appears.

**5** Tap and drag up to scroll down until the fourth box of controls appears.

**6** Tap **Default Account**.

The Default Account screen appears.

**7** Tap the account you want to make the default.

**A** A check mark appears next to the account you tapped.

**8** Tap **Mail, Contacts, Calendars**.

**Note:** To change the e-mail account for a new message, tap and hold down the **From** button, and then tap the address on the spin wheel that appears.

# Choose Alert Options for Calendar Events

B y synchronizing your calendars from your PC or Mac with your iPod touch, you can keep details of your events in the palm of your hand.

To keep yourself on schedule, you can set the iPod touch to alert you to new invitations you receive. You can also set default alert times to give you the warning you need before a regular event, an all-day event, or a birthday.

## Choose Alert Options for Calendar Events

1 Press the Home button.

2 On the Home screen, tap **Settings**.

3 On the Settings screen, tap **Mail, Contacts, Calendars**.

4 On the Mail, Contacts, Calendars screen, tap and drag up to the bottom of the screen.

5 Tap the **New Invitation Alerts** switch and move it to On or Off.

6 Tap the **Shared Calendar Alerts** switch and move it to On or Off.

7 Tap **Default Alert Times**.

8 On the Default Alert Times screen, tap the event type to set the default alert time for. For example, tap **Events**.

9 On the Events screen, Birthdays screen, or All-Day Events screen, tap the amount of time for the warning.

10 Tap **Default Alert Times**.

11 On the Default Alert Times screen, set default alert times for other event types by repeating steps **8** to **10**.

12 Tap **Mail, Contacts, Calendars**.

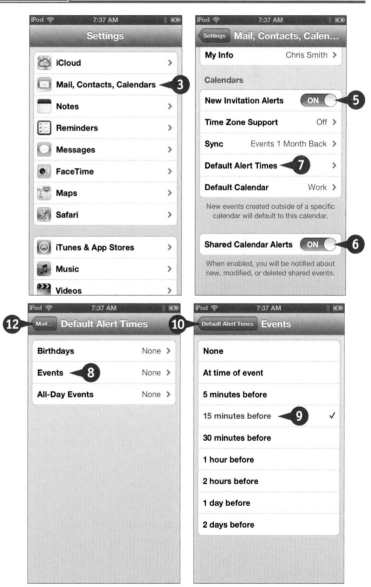

# Choose Your Default Calendar and Time Zone

When you use multiple calendars on your iPod touch, you need to set your default calendar. This is the calendar that receives events you create outside any specific calendar. For example, if you have a Work calendar and a Home calendar, you can set the Home calendar as the default calendar.

If you travel to different time zones, you may need to specify which time zone to show event dates and times in. Otherwise, Calendar uses the time zone for your current location.

## Choose Your Default Calendar and Time Zone

**1** Press the Home button.

The Home screen appears.

**2** Tap **Settings**.

The Settings screen appears.

**3** Tap and drag up to scroll down until the fourth group of buttons appears.

**4** Tap **Mail, Contacts, Calendars**.

The Mail, Contacts, Calendars screen appears.

**5** Tap and drag up to scroll down all the way to the bottom of the screen.

The bottom part of the Mail, Contacts, Calendars screen appears.

**6** Tap **Time Zone Support**.

The Time Zone Support screen appears.

**7** Tap the **Time Zone Support** switch and move it to On.

**8** Tap **Time Zone**.

The Time Zone screen appears.

**9** Type the first letters of a city in the time zone.

**10** Tap the search result you want.

**11** Tap **Time Zone Support**.

**12** Tap **Mail, Contacts, Calendars**.

**13** Tap **Default Calendar**.

The Default Calendar screen appears.

**14** Tap the calendar you want to make the default.

Ⓐ A check mark appears next to the calendar.

**15** Tap **Mail, Contacts, Calendars**.

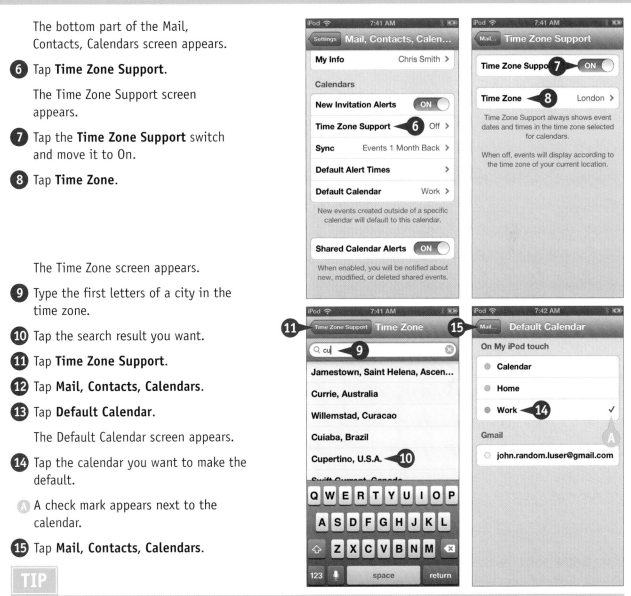

**TIP**

**How do I choose which calendars to display in the Calendar app?**
You choose the calendars in the Calendar app. Press the Home button to display the Home screen, tap **Calendar**, and then tap **Calendars**. On the Calendars screen, tap to place a check mark on each calendar you want to display. Tap to remove a check mark from a calendar you want to hide. Then tap **Done**.

As described earlier in this chapter, you can set up multiple e-mail accounts on your iPod touch. Each e-mail account can synchronize notes.

You can set the default account for notes to tell the iPod touch which e-mail account it should store new notes in unless you specify storing them elsewhere.

## Set Your Default Account for Notes

**1** Press the Home button.

The Home screen appears.

**2** Tap **Settings**.

The Settings screen appears.

**3** Scroll down to display the third group of buttons.

**4** Tap **Notes**.

The Notes screen appears.

**5** Tap **Default Account**.

**Note:** To change the font used for notes, tap **Noteworthy**, **Helvetica**, or **Marker Felt** in the Font area on the Notes screen.

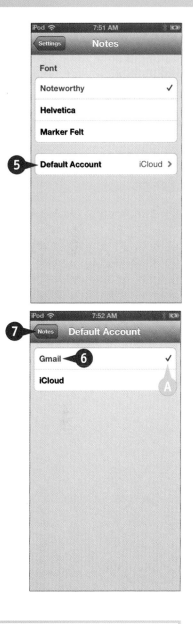

The Default Account screen appears.

**6** Tap the account you want to make the default.

**Ⓐ** A check mark appears next to the account you tapped.

**7** Tap **Notes**.

The Notes screen appears.

TIP

**Why does the Default Account setting not appear on the Notes screen on my iPod touch?**
The Default Account setting appears on the Notes screen in the Settings app when you have set up two or more e-mail accounts to synchronize notes. If you add multiple e-mail accounts to the iPod touch, but set up only one account to synchronize notes, the Default Account setting does not appear because the only Notes account is the default account.

# Send Instant Messages

When you need to communicate quickly with another person, but do not need to speak to him, you can send an instant message using the Messages app. Your iPod touch must be connected to the Internet to send and receive messages.

The Messages app runs on the iPod touch, the iPhone, the iPad, and the Mac. You can use Messages to send instant messages to other users of Messages on these devices. You can send either straightforward text messages or messages that include photos or videos.

## Send Instant Messages

1 Press the Home button.

The Home screen appears.

2 Tap **Messages**.

The Messages screen appears.

3 Tap **New Message** (✉).

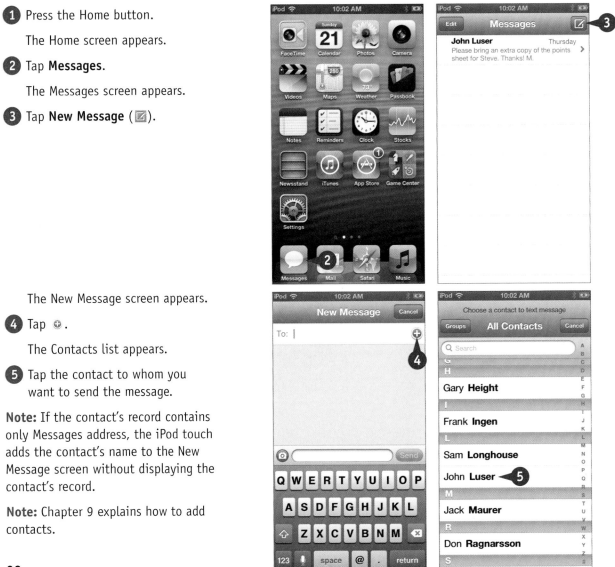

The New Message screen appears.

4 Tap ⊕.

The Contacts list appears.

5 Tap the contact to whom you want to send the message.

**Note:** If the contact's record contains only Messages address, the iPod touch adds the contact's name to the New Message screen without displaying the contact's record.

**Note:** Chapter 9 explains how to add contacts.

The contact's record opens.

**6** Tap the Messages address to use.

The contact's name appears in the To field of the New Message screen.

**7** Tap in the text field, and then type your message.

**8** To add a photo, tap .

**9** In the dialog that opens, tap **Choose Existing**. In this dialog, you can tap **Take Photo or Video** to take a photo or video with the camera (see Chapter 14), and then send it with the message.

The Photo Albums screen appears.

**10** Tap the album that contains the photo.

The album opens.

**11** Tap the photo.

The photo opens.

**12** Tap **Choose**.

The photo appears in the message.

**Note:** You can attach another photo or video by repeating steps **8** to **12**.

**13** Tap **Send**.

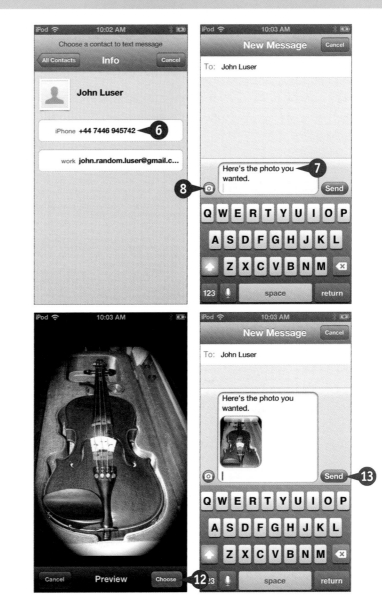

---

TIP

**Is there another way to send a photo or video?**
Yes. You can start from the Camera app or the Photos app. This way of sending a photo or video is handy when you are taking photos or videos or when you are browsing your photos or videos. Tap the photo or video you want to share, and then tap 🔄. In the dialog that opens, tap **Message**. Your iPod touch starts a message containing the photo or video. You can then address and send the message.

# Chat Face to Face Using FaceTime

By using your iPod touch's FaceTime feature, you can enjoy video chats with any of your contacts who have a fourth-generation or later iPod touch, an iPad 2 or later, an iPhone 4 or later, or a Mac running the FaceTime application.

To make a FaceTime call, you and your contact must both have Apple IDs. Your iPod touch must be connected to a wireless network so that it has an Internet connection.

## Chat Face to Face Using FaceTime

### Receive a FaceTime Call

1 When your iPod touch receives a FaceTime request, and the screen shows who is calling, aim the camera at your face, and then tap and drag the slider to answer.

A Tap ▨ if you want to turn off your video camera.

The Connecting screen appears.

When the connection is established, your iPod touch displays the caller full screen, with your video inset.

2 Start your conversation.

3 If you need to mute your microphone, tap **Mute** (▨).

B The background behind the Mute icon turns blue, and the Mute icon appears on your inset video.

4 Tap **Mute** (▨) when you want to turn muting off again.

5 Tap **End** when you are ready to end the FaceTime call.

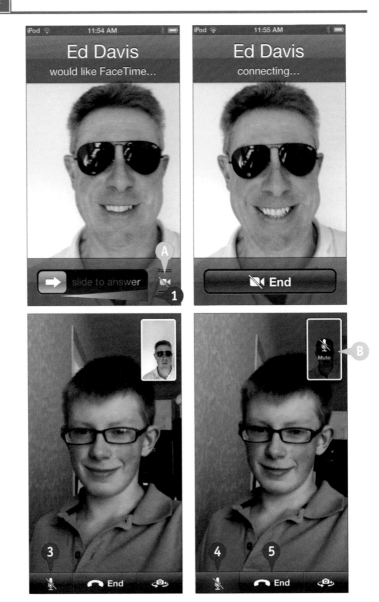

94

## Make a FaceTime Call

1 Press the Home button.

The Home screen appears.

2 Tap **FaceTime**.

The FaceTime screen appears, displaying your Contacts list.

3 Tap the contact you want to call with FaceTime.

The contact's record opens.

4 Tap **FaceTime**.

Your iPod touch starts a FaceTime call, showing your video preview.

5 When your contact answers, smile and speak.

6 If you need to show your contact something using the rear-facing camera, tap **Switch Cameras** (📷).

Ⓒ Your inset video shows the picture that is being sent to your contact.

7 When you need to switch back to showing yourself, tap **Switch Cameras** (📷).

8 When you are ready to end the call, tap **End**.

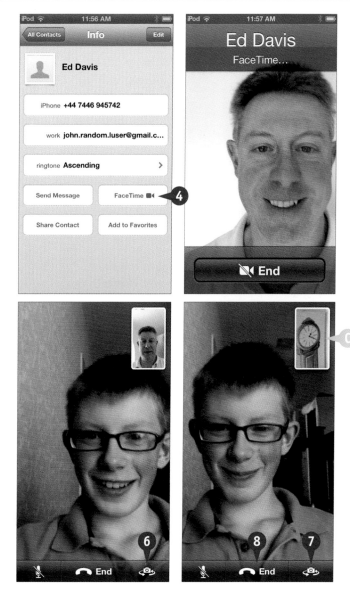

TIP

**Are there other ways of starting a FaceTime call?**

Yes. You can start a FaceTime call in two other ways:

- In the Contacts app, tap the contact to display the contact record, and then tap **FaceTime**.
- In a Messages conversation, tap **FaceTime** at the top of the screen.

# CHAPTER 6

# Connecting with Wi-Fi and Bluetooth

Your iPod touch connects to the Internet through wireless networks and Wi-Fi hotspots. It also has Bluetooth connectivity.

# Turn Wi-Fi On and Off

Normally, you will want to keep your iPod touch connected to wireless networks whenever possible so that you can make and receive FaceTime calls, send and get texts and e-mail, and access the Internet. But when you do not need or may not use Wi-Fi, you can turn on the iPod touch's Airplane Mode feature to cut off all connections.

Turning on Airplane Mode turns off Bluetooth connections as well as Wi-Fi. But you can also turn Wi-Fi on and off separately when you need to.

## Turn Wi-Fi On and Off

1 Press the Home button.

The Home screen appears.

2 Tap **Settings**.

The Settings screen appears.

3 To turn Airplane Mode on, tap the **Airplane Mode** switch and move it to the On position.

A The iPod touch turns off all Wi-Fi and Bluetooth connections. An airplane icon appears in the status bar.

4 To turn on Wi-Fi, tap **Wi-Fi**.

The Wi-Fi screen appears.

5 Tap the **Wi-Fi** switch and move it to the On position.

The list of available networks appears, and you can connect as described later in this chapter.

# Turn Bluetooth On and Off

Your iPod touch includes Bluetooth for connecting devices such as headsets, speakers, and hardware keyboards.

Bluetooth connectivity is very useful, but when you do not need it, you can turn it off to save battery power and to avoid the possibility of unwanted connections.

## Turn Bluetooth On and Off

**1** Press the Home button.

The Home screen appears.

**2** Tap **Settings**.

The Settings screen appears.

**3** Tap **Bluetooth**.

The Bluetooth screen appears.

**4** Tap the Bluetooth switch and move it to the On position or the Off position, as needed.

**5** Tap **Settings**.

The Settings screen appears again.

# Connect Bluetooth Devices to Your iPod touch

To extend your iPod touch's functionality, you can connect devices to it that communicate using the wireless Bluetooth technology.

For example, you can connect a Bluetooth headset and microphone so that you can listen to music and make and take FaceTime calls. Or you can connect a Bluetooth keyboard so that you can quickly type e-mail messages, notes, or documents.

## Connect Bluetooth Devices to Your iPod touch

### Set Up a Bluetooth Device

**1** Press the Home button.

The Home screen appears.

**2** Tap **Settings**.

The Settings screen appears.

**3** Tap **Bluetooth**.

The Bluetooth screen appears.

**4** Tap the **Bluetooth** switch and move it to On.

**A** The Devices list appears, and the iPod touch scans for Bluetooth devices.

**5** Turn on the Bluetooth device and make it discoverable.

**Note:** Read the Bluetooth device's instructions to find out how to make the device discoverable via Bluetooth.

**B** The Bluetooth device appears in the Devices list, marked Not Paired.

**6** Tap the device's button.

The iPod touch pairs with the device, and then connects to it.

**C** The Devices list shows the device as Connected.

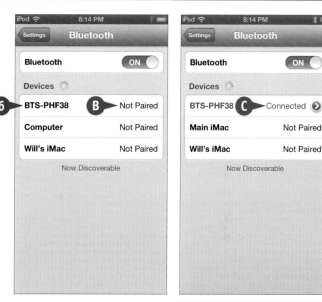

## Choose the Device for Playing Audio or Taking a Call

**1** When you start playing music or receive a FaceTime call, your iPod touch displays a dialog for choosing which device to use. Tap the button for the device you want.

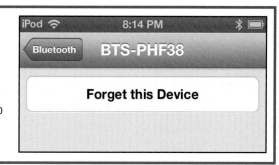

### TIP

**How do I stop using a Bluetooth device?**

When you no longer need to use a particular Bluetooth device, tell your iPod touch to forget it. Press the Home button, tap **Settings**, and then tap **General**. On the General screen, tap **Bluetooth**, and then tap the device's ⊘ button. On the device's screen, tap **Forget this Device**, and then tap **Forget Device** in the confirmation dialog.

Your iPod touch can connect to the Internet via Wi-Fi networks. The first time you connect to a Wi-Fi network, you must provide the network's password. After that, the iPod touch stores the password, so you can connect to the network without entering the password again.

## Connect to Wi-Fi Networks

**1** Press the Home button.

The Home screen appears.

**A** The Wi-Fi signal icon ( 🛜 ) in the status bar and on the Wi-Fi screen shows the strength of the Wi-Fi signal. The more bars that appear, the stronger the signal is.

**2** Tap **Settings**.

The Settings screen appears.

**3** Tap **Wi-Fi**.

The Wi-Fi screen appears.

**4** If Wi-Fi is off, tap the **Wi-Fi** switch and move it to On.

The Choose a Network list appears. A lock icon ( 🔒 ) indicates the network has security such as a password.

**5** Tap the network you want to connect to.

**Note:** If the network does not have a password, your iPod touch connects to it without prompting you for a password.

**6** On the Enter Password screen, type the password.

**7** Tap **Join**.

Your iPod touch connects to the wireless network.

**Ⓑ** The Wi-Fi screen appears again, showing a check mark next to the network the iPod touch has connected to.

**Note:** To stop your iPod touch from connecting to a particular wireless network, tap ⊘ to the right of the network's name on the Wi-Fi screen. On the network's screen, tap **Forget this Network**. In the dialog that opens, tap **Forget**.

**8** Tap **Settings**.

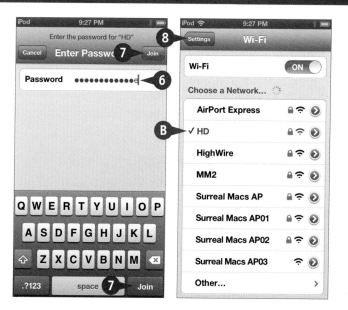

## TIP

**How do I connect to a network not listed on the Wi-Fi screen?**

If a wireless network is not broadcasting its network name, the network does not appear on the Wi-Fi screen. Follow these steps:

**1** From the Wi-Fi screen, tap **Other**.

**2** On the Other Network screen, type the network name.

**3** Tap **Security**.

**4** On the Security screen, tap the security type — for example, **WPA2**.

**5** Tap **Other Network**.

**6** Type the password in the Password box on the Other Network screen.

**7** Tap **Join**.

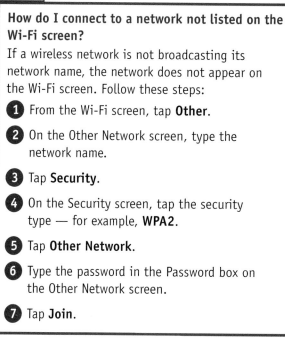

# Log In to Wi-Fi Hotspots

When you are in town or on the road, you can log in to Wi-Fi hotspots to get Internet access so that you can use Mail, Messages, FaceTime, and other features that require the Internet.

You can find Wi-Fi hotspots at many locations, including coffee shops and restaurants, hotels, and airports. Some municipal areas, and even some parks and highway rest stops, also provide public Wi-Fi. Some Wi-Fi hotspots charge for access, whereas others are free to use.

## Log In to Wi-Fi Hotspots

**1** Press the Home button.

The Home screen appears.

**2** Tap **Settings**.

The Settings screen appears.

**3** Tap **Wi-Fi**.

The Wi-Fi screen appears.

**4** If Wi-Fi is off, tap the **Wi-Fi** switch and move it to On.

The list of wireless networks appears.

**5** Tap the Wi-Fi hotspot you want to join.

**Note:** If the iPod touch prompts you to enter a username and password, enter those the hotspot operator has given you. Many Wi-Fi hotspots use a login page instead of a username and password.

**Ⓐ** The iPod touch joins the hotspot. The Wi-Fi screen displays a check mark next to the hotspot.

**⑥** If Safari opens and displays a login page, type the login information for the hotspot, and then tap the button for logging in.

After connecting to the hotspot, you can use the Internet. For example, you can browse the web using Safari or send and receive e-mail using the Mail app.

## TIP

**What precautions should I take when using Wi-Fi hotspots?**

The main danger is that you may connect to a malevolent network.

To stay safe, connect only to hotspots provided by reputable establishments — for example, national hotel chains or restaurant chains — instead of hotspots run by unknown operators.

When you finish using a Wi-Fi hotspot that you do not plan to use again, tell the iPod touch to forget the network using the technique described in the previous task.

Forgetting the network avoids this problem: After you have connected the iPod touch to a wireless network, it will connect to another network that has the same name, security type, and password, even if that network is not the same network. This feature normally saves time, but it also enables an imposter to set up a fake hotspot that pretends to be a genuine hotspot you have previously used.

# CHAPTER 7

# Working with Apps

In this chapter, you first learn to customize the Home screen, putting the icons you need most right to hand and organizing them into folders. You then grasp how to switch instantly among the apps you are running, how to find the apps you need on Apple's App Store, and how to update and remove apps.

# Customize the Home Screen

From the Home screen, you run the apps on your iPod touch. You can customize the Home screen to put the apps you use most frequently within easy reach. When the first Home screen fills up with icons, the iPod touch adds further Home screens automatically and populates them with apps you add. You can also create further Home screens as needed and move the app icons among them. You can customize the Home screen by working on the iPod touch, as described here. If you synchronize your iPod touch with a computer, you can use iTunes instead. This is an easier way to make extensive changes.

## Customize the Home Screen

### Unlock the Icons for Customization

**1** Press the Home button.

The Home screen appears.

**2** Tap and drag left or right to display the Home screen you want to customize.

**A** You can also tap the dot for the Home screen you want to display.

**3** Tap and hold the icon you want to move.

**Note:** You can tap and hold any icon until the apps start jiggling. Usually, it is easiest to tap and hold the icon you want to move, and then drag the icon.

The icons start to jiggle, indicating that you can move them.

### Move an Icon within a Home Screen

**1** After unlocking the icons, drag the icon to where you want it.

The other icons move out of the way.

**2** When the icon is in the right place, drop it.

The icon stays in its new position.

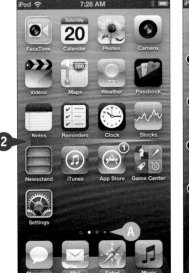

## Move an Icon to a Different Home Screen

**1** After unlocking the icons, drag the icon to the left edge of the screen to display the previous Home screen or to the right edge to display the next Home screen.

The previous Home screen or next Home screen appears.

**2** Drag the icon to where you want it.

The other icons move out of the way.

**3** Drop the icon.

The icon stays in its new position.

## Stop Customizing the Home Screen

**1** Press the Home button.

The icons stop jiggling.

## TIPS

**How can I put the default apps back on the Home screen?**

Press the Home button, tap **Settings**, and then tap **General**. Tap and drag up to scroll down the screen, and then tap **Reset**. On the Reset screen, tap **Reset Home Screen Layout**, and then tap **Reset Home Screen** () in the dialog that opens. Press the Home button to return to the Home screen.

**I have too many apps to navigate easily. Is there an easy fix?**

Yes. You can create folders as discussed in the next task, and then put the apps into the folders.

# Organize Apps with Folders

To organize the Home screen, you can arrange the items into folders. The iPod touch's default Home screen layout includes a folder named Utilities, but you can create as many other folders as you need.

You create a folder by dragging one icon onto another icon. Doing this creates a folder containing both items. You can then rename the folder.

## Organize Apps with Folders

### Create a Folder

**1** Display the Home screen that contains the item you want to put into a folder.

**2** Tap and hold the item until the icons start to jiggle.

**Note:** When creating a folder, you may find it easiest to first put both the items you will add to the folder on the same screen.

**3** Drag the item to the other icon you want to place in the folder you create.

The iPod touch creates a folder, puts both icons in it, and assigns a default name based on the genre.

**4** Tap ⊗ in the folder name box.

The keyboard appears.

**5** Type the name for the folder.

**6** Tap outside the folder.

The iPod touch applies the name to the folder.

## Open an Item in a Folder

 Display the Home screen that contains the folder.

**2** Tap the folder's icon.

The folder's contents appear, and the items outside the folder fade.

**3** Tap the item you want to open.

The item opens.

## Add an Item to a Folder

**1** Display the Home screen that contains the item.

**2** Tap and hold the item until the icons start to jiggle.

**3** Drag the icon on top of the folder and drop it there.

**Note:** If the folder is on a different Home screen from the icon, drag the icon to the left edge to display the previous Home screen or to the right edge to display the next Home screen.

The item goes into the folder.

**4** Press the Home button to stop the icons jiggling.

### How do I take an item out of a folder?

**1** Tap the folder to display its contents.

**2** Tap and hold the item until the icons start to jiggle.

**3** Drag the item out of the folder. The folder closes and the Home screen appears.

**4** Drag the item to where you want it, and then drop it.

# Switch Quickly from One App to Another

The most straightforward way of switching from one app to another is to press the Home button to display the Home screen, and then tap the icon for the app you want to start using. But the iPod touch also has an app-switching bar that enables you to switch quickly from one running app to another running app without needing to display the Home screen.

## Switch Quickly from One App to Another

**1** Press the Home button.

The Home screen appears.

**2** Tap the app you want to launch.

The app's screen appears.

**3** Start using the app as usual.

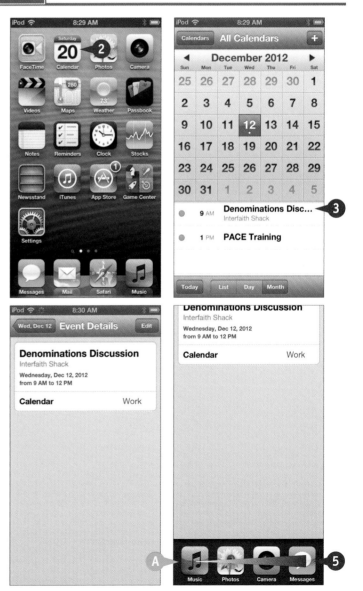

**4** Press the Home button twice in quick succession.

**A** The app-switching bar appears.

**5** Tap and drag left or right to scroll the app-switching bar until you see the app you want.

**6** Tap the app in the app-switching bar.

The app appears.

**7** When you are ready to switch back, press the Home button twice in quick succession.

The app-switching bar appears.

**8** Tap the app to which you want to return.

The app appears, ready to resume from where you stopped using it.

### How do I stop an app that is not responding?

If an app stops responding, you can quickly close it from the app-switching bar. Press the Home button twice to open the app-switching bar. Tap and hold the app that has stopped responding (Ⓐ). Tap ⊖ on the app to close the app (Ⓑ). Press the Home button or tap the screen above the app-switching bar to hide ⊖.

# Find the Apps You Need on the App Store

The iPod touch comes with essential apps, such as Safari for surfing the web, Mail for e-mail, and Calendar for keeping your schedule. But to get the most out of your iPod touch, you will likely need to add other apps.

To get apps, you use the App Store, which provides apps that Apple has approved as correctly programmed, suitable for purpose, and not containing malevolent code. Before you can download any apps, including free apps, you must create an App Store account.

## Find the Apps You Need on the App Store

1. Press the Home button.

   The Home screen appears.

2. Tap **App Store**.

   The App Store screen appears.

3. Tap **Categories**.

   The Categories screen appears.

4. Tap the category you want to see.

   The category screen appears, showing the New list and the What's Hot list.

5. Tap and drag to see further apps in a list, or tap and drag up to see other lists. Then tap **See All** to display your chosen list.

The screen shows the list you chose.

 **6** Tap the app you want to view.

The app's screen appears.

**Note:** To understand what an app does and how well it does it, look at the app's rating, read the description, and read the user reviews.

**7** Tap the price button or the **Free** button.

The price button or Free button changes to an Install App button.

 **8** Tap **Install App**.

**9** If the iPod touch prompts you to sign in, type your password and tap **OK**.

**Note:** If you have not created an App Store account already, the iPod touch prompts you to create one now.

The iPod touch downloads and installs the app.

 **10** Tap **Open** to launch the app.

---

**TIP**

**Why does the App Store not appear on the Home screen or when I search?**
If the App Store does not appear on the Home screen, and if searching for it does not show a result, the iPod touch has restrictions applied that prevent you from installing apps. You can remove these restrictions if you know the restrictions passcode. Press the Home button, tap **Settings**, and then tap **General**. Scroll down, and then tap **Restrictions**. Type the passcode on the Enter Passcode screen, and then tap the **Installing Apps** switch and move it to On.

# Update and Remove Apps

To keep your iPod touch's apps running well, you should install app updates when they become available. Most updates for paid apps are free, but you must usually pay to upgrade to a new version of the app. You can download and install updates using either iTunes or the iPod touch.

When you no longer need an app, you can remove it from the iPod touch.

## Update and Remove Apps

### Update an App

1 In iTunes, click **Apps**.

The Apps list appears.

2 Click **Check for Updates**.

iTunes displays the Sign In to Download from the iTunes Store dialog.

3 Type your password.

4 Click **Sign In**.

The My App Updates screen appears.

5 Click **Download All Free Updates**.

iTunes downloads the updates.

6 Connect the iPod touch if it is not already connected.

7 If the iPod touch does not sync automatically, click **Sync** to start synchronization.

## Remove an App from the iPod touch

**1** Press the Home button.

The Home screen appears.

**2** Display the Home screen that contains the app you want to delete.

**3** Tap and hold the item until the icons start to jiggle.

**4** Tap  on the icon.

The Delete dialog appears.

**5** Tap **Delete**.

The iPod touch deletes the app, and the app's icon disappears.

---

### TIP

**Can I update an app on the iPod touch as well?**
Yes. To update an app on the iPod touch, press the Home button. The badge on the App Store icon (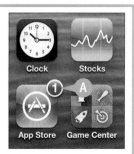) shows the number of available updates. Tap **App Store**, tap **Updates**, and then tap **Update All**. Type your password in the Apple ID Password dialog, and then tap **OK**. The iPod touch then downloads and installs the updates. The icons on the Updates screen show the progress of the updates.

# CHAPTER 8

# Browsing the Web and Sending E-Mail

**Your iPod touch is fully equipped to browse the web and send e-mail via a Wi-Fi connection.**

# Browse the Web with Safari

Your iPod touch comes equipped with the Safari app, which you use for browsing the web. You can quickly go to a web page by entering its address in the Address box or by following a link.

Although you can browse quickly by opening a single web page at a time, you may prefer to open multiple pages and switch back and forth among them. Safari makes this easy to do.

## Browse the Web with Safari

### Open Safari and Navigate to Web Pages

**1** Press the Home button.

The Home screen appears.

**2** Tap **Safari**.

Safari opens and loads the last web page that was shown.

**3** Tap the Address box.

The Address box expands, and the keyboard appears.

**4** Tap ⊗ if you need to delete the contents of the Address box.

**5** Type the address of the page you want to open.

**6** Tap **Go**.

**Note:** You can also tap a search result that Safari displays below the Address box.

Safari displays the page.

**7** Tap a link on the page.

Safari displays that page.

**A** After going to a new page, tap ◄ to display the previous page. You can then tap ► to go forward again to the page you just went back from.

## Open Multiple Pages and Navigate Among Them

**1** Tap **Pages** ().

Safari shrinks the current page and displays a Close button (⊗).

**2** Tap **New Page**.

Safari opens a blank page and expands it to full screen.

**3** Tap the Address box, and then go to the page you want.

**Note:** You can also go to a page by using a bookmark, as described in the next task.

The page appears.

**Ⓑ** The Pages button shows the number of pages open.

**4** To switch to another page, tap **Pages** (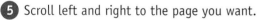).

Safari shrinks the current page and displays a Close button (⊗).

**5** Scroll left and right to the page you want.

**6** Tap the page you want to see.

**Ⓒ** You can tap the **Close** button (⊗) to close a page.

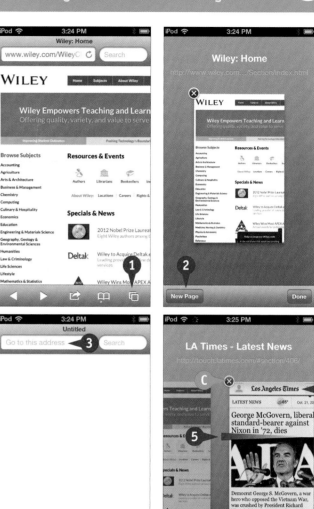

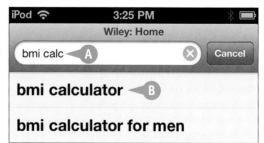

**How do I search for information?**

Tap the Search box to display the Search screen, and then type your search terms (Ⓐ). Safari searches as you type; you can type further to narrow down the results, and stop as soon as you see suitable results. Tap the result you want to see (Ⓑ), and then tap a link on the results page that Safari opens.

# Access Websites Quickly with Your Bookmarks

Typing web addresses can be laborious, even with the help the iPod touch's keyboard adds, so you will probably want to use bookmarks to access websites you value.

By syncing your existing bookmarks from your PC or Mac, as described in Chapter 2, you can instantly provide your iPod touch with quick access to the web pages you want to visit most frequently. You can also create bookmarks on your iPod touch, as discussed in the next task.

**Access Websites Quickly with Your Bookmarks**

### Open the Bookmarks Screen

**1** Press the Home button.

The Home screen appears.

**2** Tap **Safari**.

Safari opens.

**3** Tap **Bookmarks** ( ).

The Bookmarks screen appears.

### Explore Your History

**1** On the Bookmarks screen, tap **History**.

A list of the web pages you have recently visited appears.

**Ⓐ** Tap a day to display the list of web pages you visited on that day.

**2** Tap **Bookmarks** to return to the Bookmarks screen.

## Explore a Bookmarks Category

**1** On the Bookmarks screen, tap the bookmarks folder or category you want to see. For example, tap **Bookmarks Bar**.

The contents of the folder or category appear. For example, the contents of the Bookmarks Bar folder appear.

**2** Tap the item you want to view. For example, tap **News**.

The item appears — for example, the News screen appears.

**3** Tap the button in the upper left corner one or more times to go back. For example, tap **Bookmarks** to return to the Bookmarks screen.

## Open a Bookmarked Page

**1** When you find the bookmark for the web page you want to open, tap the bookmark.

**B** The web page opens.

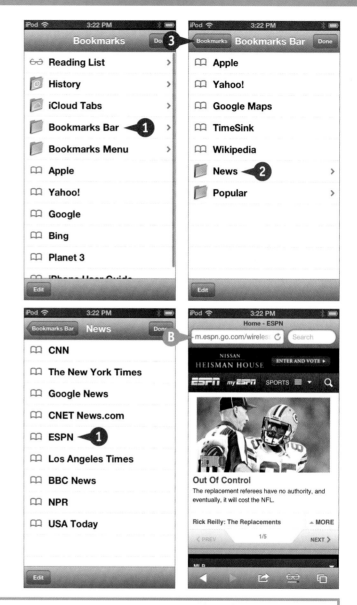

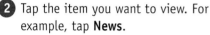

## TIP

**How can I quickly access a website?**

Creating a bookmark within Safari is good for sites you access now and then, but if you access a site frequently, create an icon for it on your Home screen. Tap **Share** (⬆), tap **Add to Home Screen** (**A**), type the name on the Add to Home screen, and then tap **Add**. You can then go straight to the page by tapping its icon on the Home screen.

# Create Bookmarks and Share Web Pages

While browsing the web on your iPod touch, you will likely find web pages you want to access again. To access such a web page easily, create a bookmark for it. If you have set your iPod touch to sync bookmarks with your computer, the bookmark becomes available on your computer, too, when you sync. You can also add a web page to your Reading List so that you can access it again quickly.

To share a web page with other people, you can quickly send the page's address via e-mail.

## Create Bookmarks and Share Web Pages

### Create a Bookmark on the iPod touch

1 Press the Home button.

The Home screen appears.

2 Tap **Safari**.

Safari opens and displays the last web page you were viewing.

3 Navigate to the web page you want to bookmark.

4 Tap **Share** ().

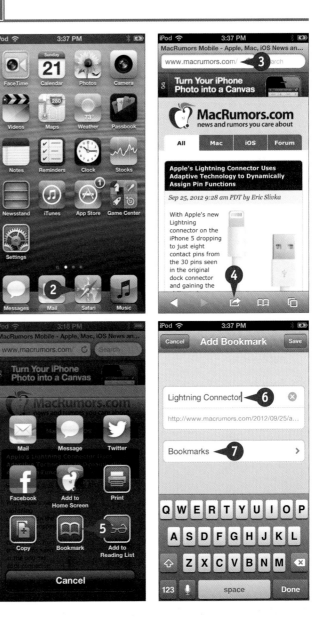

The Share screen opens.

5 Tap **Bookmark**.

**Note:** To add the web page to your Reading List, tap **Add to Reading List** on the Share screen.

The Add Bookmark screen appears.

6 Edit the suggested name, or type a new name.

7 Tap the **Bookmarks** button.

The Bookmarks screen appears.

**8** Tap the folder you want to create the bookmark in.

The Add Bookmark screen appears again.

**9** Tap **Save**.

Safari creates the bookmark.

## Share a Web Page's Address via E-Mail

**1** In Safari, navigate to the web page whose address you want to share.

**2** Tap **Share** (⬆).

The Share screen appears.

**3** Tap **Mail**.

The iPod touch starts a new message in the Mail app and adds the link to it.

**4** Add the address by typing or by tapping ⊕ and choosing it from your Contacts list.

**5** Edit the suggested subject line if necessary.

**6** Type any explanatory text needed.

**7** Tap **Send**.

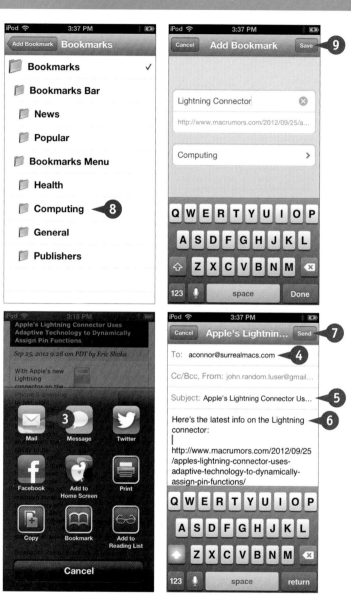

---

**Can I change a bookmark I have created?**

Yes. Tap 📖 to display the Bookmarks screen, and then navigate to the bookmark you want to change. Tap **Edit** to display a button for opening a bookmark to change it and controls for deleting bookmarks and changing their order.

**How do I access my Reading List?**

Tap 📖 to display the Bookmarks screen, and then tap **Reading List** to display the Reading List screen. You can then tap the web page you want to view.

# Configure Your Default Search Engine

To find information with Safari, you often need to search using a search engine. Safari's default search engine is Google, but you can change to another search engine. Your choices are Google, Yahoo!, and Bing.

Google, Yahoo!, and Bing compete directly with one another and return similar results to many searches. But if you experiment with the three search engines, you will gradually discover which one suits you best.

## Configure Your Default Search Engine

**1** Press the Home button.

The Home screen appears.

**2** Tap **Settings**.

The Settings screen appears.

**3** Tap and drag up to scroll down the screen until the fourth box appears.

**4** Tap **Safari**.

The Safari screen appears.

**5** Tap **Search Engine**.

The Search Engine screen appears.

 Tap the search engine you want — for example, **Yahoo!**.

A check mark appears next to the search engine you tapped.

**7** Tap **Safari**.

**A** The Safari screen appears again, now showing the search engine you chose.

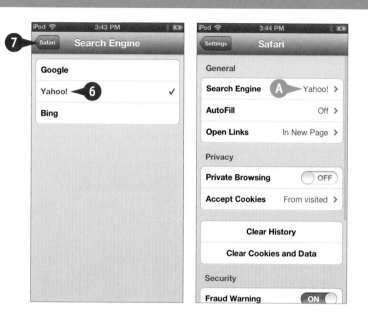

**How can I search using a search engine other than Google, Yahoo!, or Bing?**

You can search using any search engine you can find on the web. Open a web page to the search engine, and then perform the search using the tools on the page. At this writing, you cannot set any search engine other than Google, Yahoo!, or Bing as the iPod touch's default search engine. Instead, either add the site to your Bookmarks bar or create a link on your Home screen to the site.

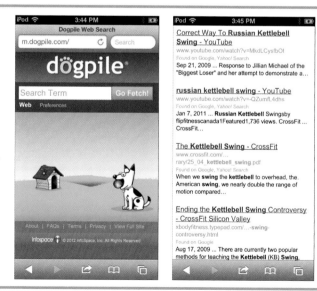

# Fill in Forms Quickly with AutoFill

If you fill in forms using your iPod touch, you can save time by enabling the AutoFill feature. AutoFill can automatically fill in standard form fields, such as name and address fields, using the information from a contact card you specify.

AutoFill can also automatically store other data you enter in fields, and can store usernames and passwords to enter them for you automatically. For security, you may prefer not to store your usernames and passwords with AutoFill.

## Fill in Forms Quickly with AutoFill

 Press the Home button.

The Home screen appears.

 Tap **Settings**.

The Settings screen appears.

 Tap and drag up to scroll down the screen until the fourth box appears.

 Tap **Safari**.

The Safari screen appears.

 Tap **AutoFill**.

The AutoFill screen appears.

**6** Tap the **Use Contact Info** switch and move it to On.

**7** Tap **My Info**.

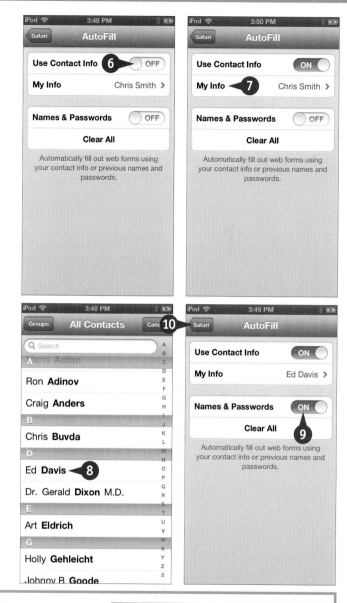

The Contacts screen appears.

**8** Tap the contact card that contains the information you want to use.

The AutoFill screen appears again, with the name you chose in the My Info area.

**9** Tap the **Names & Passwords** switch and move it to On.

**10** Tap **Safari**.

The Safari screen appears again.

## TIP

**When should I clear my AutoFill information?**
Clear your AutoFill information if you want to remove stored usernames and passwords from your iPod touch, or if AutoFill has stored incorrect information that you have entered in forms. To clear your AutoFill information, tap **Clear All** on the AutoFill screen, and then tap **Clear AutoFill Data** (Ⓐ) in the confirmation dialog that opens.

# Tighten Up Safari's Security

A long with its many and varied sites that provide useful information or services, the web contains sites that try to infect computers with malevolent software, or *malware*, or lure visitors into providing sensitive personal or financial information. Although Apple has built the iPod touch and Safari to be as secure as possible, it is wise to choose high-security settings. This task shows you how to turn on the Fraud Warning feature, block JavaScript and pop-ups, and choose which cookies to accept.

## Tighten Up Safari's Security

**1** Press the Home button.

The Home screen appears.

**2** Tap **Settings**.

The Settings screen appears.

**3** Tap and drag up to scroll down the screen until the fourth box appears.

**4** Tap **Safari**.

The Safari screen appears.

**5** Tap and drag up to scroll down the screen until the bottom of the screen appears.

**6** Tap the **Fraud Warning** switch and move it to On.

**Note:** The Fraud Warning warns you when you try to open a site on a blacklist of offending sites. This feature is not infallible, but it is helpful.

**7** Tap the **JavaScript** switch and move it to Off.

**Note:** JavaScript is used to provide extra features on web pages. Because JavaScript can be used to attack your iPod touch, disabling JavaScript is the safest option. The disadvantage is that disabling JavaScript may remove some or most functionality of harmless sites.

**8** Tap the **Block Pop-ups** switch and move it to On.

**Note:** A pop-up is an extra web page that opens automatically. Some pop-ups attempt to show information most visitors do not want to see.

⑨ Tap and drag down to scroll up the screen a little way so that you can see the Privacy section.

⑩ Tap **Accept Cookies**.

The Accept Cookies screen appears. See the tip for an explanation of cookies.

⑪ Tap **From visited**.

⑫ Tap **Safari**.

The Safari screen appears again.

⑬ If you want to clear your browsing history, tap **Clear History**, and then tap **Clear History** in the dialog that opens.

⑭ If you want to clear your cookies and cached data, tap **Clear Cookies and Data**, and then tap **Clear Cookies and Data** in the dialog box that opens.

**What are cookies, and what threat do they pose?**
A cookie is a small text file that a website places on a computer to identify that computer in the future. This is helpful for many sites, such as shopping sites in which you add items to a shopping cart, but when used by malevolent sites, cookies can pose a threat to your privacy. You can set Safari to never accept cookies, but this prevents many legitimate websites from working properly. So accepting cookies only from sites you visit is normally the best compromise.

# Read Your E-Mail Messages

After you have set up Mail by synchronizing accounts from your computer, as described in Chapter 2, or by configuring accounts manually on the iPod touch, as described in Chapter 5, you are ready to send and receive e-mail messages using your iPod touch.

This task shows you how to read your incoming e-mail messages. You learn to reply to messages and write messages from scratch later in this chapter.

## Read Your E-Mail Messages

 **1** Press the Home button.

The Home screen appears.

**2** Tap **Mail**.

The Mail screen appears.

**Note:** If Mail does not show the Mailboxes screen, tap the button in the upper left corner until the Mailboxes screen appears.

**3** Tap the inbox you want to see.

**A** To see all your incoming messages together, tap **All Inboxes**. Depending on how you use e-mail, you may find seeing all your messages at once helpful.

The inbox opens.

**B** A blue dot to the left of a message indicates that you have not read the message yet.

**C** A blue star to the left of a message indicates the message is from a VIP. See the second tip for information about VIPs.

**4** Tap the message you want to open.

The message opens.

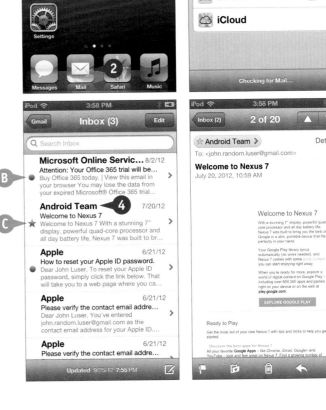

⑤ Turn the iPod touch sideways if you want to view the message in landscape orientation.

In landscape orientation, you can see the message at a larger size, so it is easier to read.

⑥ Tap 🔽.

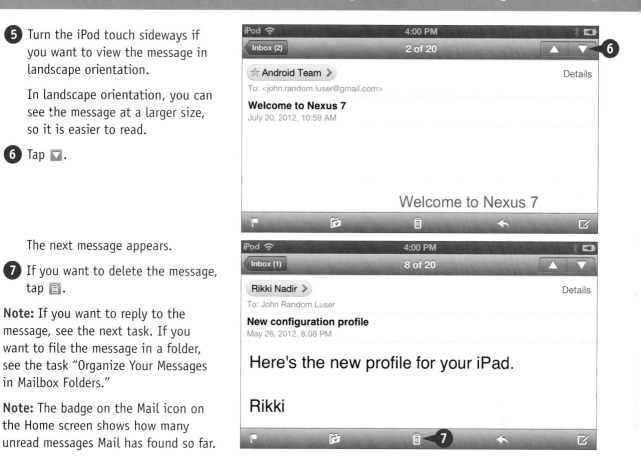

The next message appears.

⑦ If you want to delete the message, tap 🗑.

**Note:** If you want to reply to the message, see the next task. If you want to file the message in a folder, see the task "Organize Your Messages in Mailbox Folders."

**Note:** The badge on the Mail icon on the Home screen shows how many unread messages Mail has found so far.

**How do I view the contents of another mailbox?**
From an open message, tap **Inbox** or **All Inboxes** to return to the inbox or the screen for all the inboxes. Tap **Mailboxes** to go back to the Mailboxes screen. You can then tap the mailbox you want to view.

**What is the VIP inbox on the Mailboxes screen?**
The VIP inbox is a tool for identifying important messages, no matter which e-mail account they come to. You mark particular contacts as being very important people to you, and Mail then adds messages from these VIPs to the VIP inbox. To add a VIP, tap **VIP** on the Mailboxes screen, tap **Add VIP** on the VIP List screen, and then tap the contact in the Contacts list.

# Reply To or Forward an E-Mail Message

After receiving an e-mail message, you often need to reply to it. You can choose between replying only to the sender of the message and replying to the sender and all the other recipients in the To field and the Cc field, if there are any. Recipients in the message's Bcc field, whose names you cannot see, do not receive your reply.

Other times, you may need to forward a message you have received to one or more other people. The Mail app makes both replying and forwarding messages as easy as possible.

## Reply To or Forward an E-Mail Message

### Open the Message You Will Reply To or Forward

**1** Press the Home button.

The Home screen appears.

**2** Tap **Mail**.

The Mailboxes screen appears.

**Note:** When you launch Mail, the app checks for new messages. This is why the number of new messages you see on the Mailboxes screen may differ from the number on the Mail badge on the Home screen.

**3** Tap the inbox you want to see.

The inbox opens.

**4** Tap the message you want to open.

The message opens.

**5** Tap **Action** (⬅).

The Action menu opens.

**Note:** You can also reply to or forward a message by using Siri. For example, say "Reply to this message" or "Forward this message to Alice Smith," and then tell Siri what you want the message to say.

## Reply to the Message

**1** In the Action menu, tap **Reply**.

**A** To reply to all recipients, tap **Reply All**. Reply to all recipients only when you are sure that they need to receive your reply. Often, it is better to reply only to the sender.

A screen containing the reply appears.

**2** Type your reply to the message.

**3** Tap **Send**.

Mail sends the message.

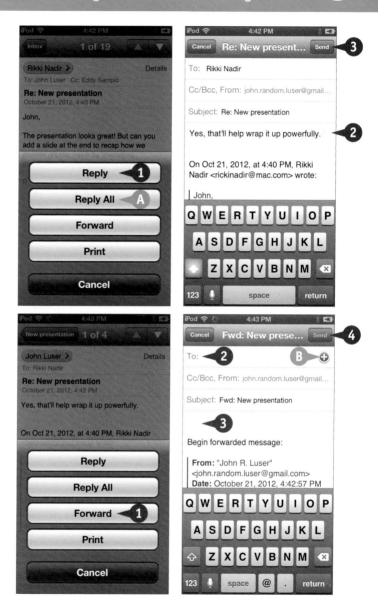

## Forward the Message

**1** In the Action menu, tap **Forward**.

A screen containing the forwarded message appears.

**2** Type the recipient's address.

**B** Alternatively, you can tap ⊕ and choose the recipient in your Contacts list.

**3** Type a message if needed.

**4** Tap **Send**.

Mail sends the message.

## TIP

### How do I check for new messages?

In a mailbox, tap and drag your finger down the screen. A curling refresh arrow appears at the top of the screen. Drag further so that the circle becomes a teardrop, and keep dragging. When the teardrop explodes, Mail checks for new messages.

# Organize Your Messages in Mailbox Folders

To keep your inbox or inboxes under control, you should organize your messages into mailbox folders.

You can quickly move a single message to a folder after reading it, or you can select multiple messages in your inbox and move them all to a folder in a single action.

## Organize Your Messages in Mailbox Folders

### Open Your Inbox

▶ Press the Home button.

The Home screen appears.

▶ Tap **Mail**.

The Mailboxes screen appears.

**3** Tap the inbox you want to open.

The inbox opens.

### Move a Single Message to a Folder

▶ Tap the message you want to read.

The message opens.

▶ Tap **Folders** (📁).

The Mailboxes screen appears.

③ Tap the mailbox to which you want to move the message.

Mail moves the message.

The next message in the inbox appears, so that you can read it and file it if necessary.

## Move Multiple Messages to a Folder

① In the inbox, tap **Edit**.

An empty selection button appears to the left of each message, and the Delete button and Move button appear.

② Tap the selection button (●) next to each message you want to move.

③ Tap **Move**.

The Mailboxes screen appears.

④ Tap the mailbox to which you want to move the messages.

Mail moves the messages.

Your inbox then appears again, so that you can work with other messages.

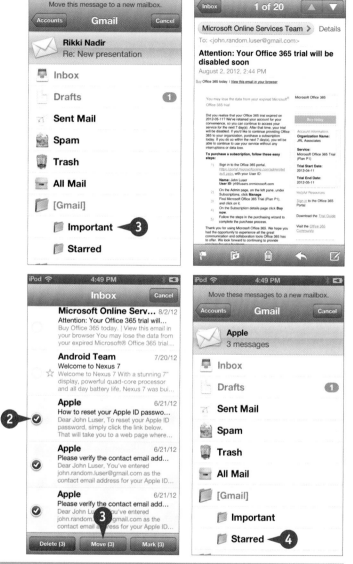

**TIP**

**Can I move messages from an inbox in one account to a mailbox in another account?**

Yes. In the inbox, tap **Edit**, and then tap the selection button (●) for each message you want to affect. Tap **Move**, and then tap **Accounts**. On the Accounts screen, tap the account (Ⓐ) that contains the mailbox to which you want to move the messages, and then tap the mailbox.

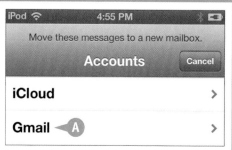

# Write and Send E-Mail Messages

Your iPod touch is great for reading and replying to e-mail messages you receive, but you will likely also need to write new messages. When you do, you can use the data in the Contacts app to address your outgoing messages quickly and accurately. If the recipient's address is not one of your contacts, you can type the address manually.

You can attach one or more files to an e-mail message to send those files to the recipient. This works well for small files, but many mail servers reject files larger than several megabytes in size.

## Write and Send E-Mail Messages

① Press the Home button.

The Home screen appears.

② Tap **Mail**.

The Mailboxes screen appears.

③ Tap **New Message** ().

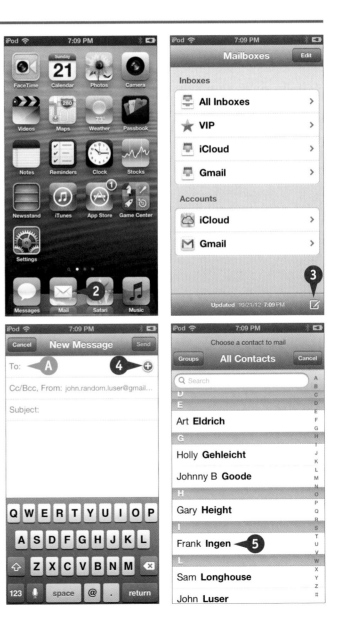

The New Message screen appears.

④ Tap ⊕.

The Contacts list appears.

**Note:** If necessary, change the Contacts list displayed by tapping **Groups**, making your choice on the Groups screen, and then tapping **Done**.

Ⓐ If the person you are e-mailing is not a contact, type the address in the To area. You can also start typing here and then select a matching contact from the list that the Mail app displays.

⑤ Tap the contact you want to send the message to.

The contact's name appears as a button in the To area.

**Note:** You can add other contacts to the To area by repeating steps **4** and **5**.

⑥ If you need to add a Cc or Bcc recipient, tap **Cc/Bcc, From**.

The Cc, Bcc, and From fields expand.

⑦ Tap the Cc area or Bcc area, and then follow steps **4** and **5** to add a recipient.

To change the e-mail account you are sending the message from, tap **From**, and then tap the account to use.

⑧ Tap **Subject**, and then type the message's subject.

⑨ Tap below the Subject line, and then type the body of the message.

⑩ Tap **Send**.

Mail sends the message.

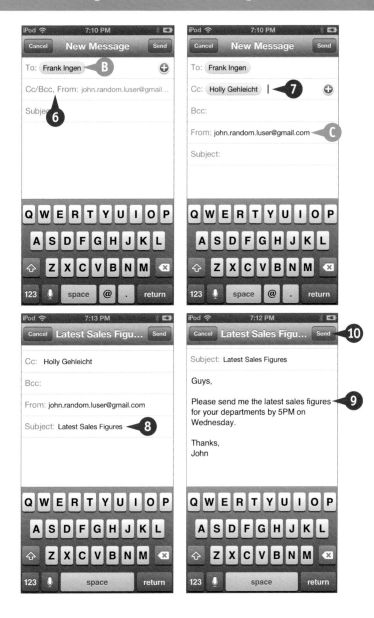

**TIP**

**How do I attach a file to a message?**
To attach a file to the message, start the message from the app that contains the file. For example, to send a photo, open the Photos app. Select the photo, tap **Share** (⬆), and then tap **Mail**. Mail starts a message with the photo attached. You then address the message and send it.

# View Files Attached to Incoming E-Mail Messages

-mail is not just a great way to communicate, but you can use it to transfer files quickly and easily. When you receive an e-mail message with a file attached to it, you can quickly view the file from the Mail app.

When you receive an e-mail message that has a small file attached, the Mail app automatically downloads the whole file. If the attachment is a large file, the Mail app downloads part of it, and you must tap the attachment to download the rest of it. This behavior helps avoid filling the iPod touch with large files you do not want.

## View Files Attached to Incoming E-Mail Messages

1 Press the Home button.

The Home screen appears.

2 Tap **Mail**.

The Mailboxes screen appears.

3 Tap the inbox you want to open.

The inbox opens.

A A paperclip icon (  ) indicates that a message has one or more files attached.

4 Tap the message you want to open.

The message opens.

5 If the attachment appears as an outline with a Download button ( ↓ ), tap to download the attachment.

A button for the attachment appears.

**6** Tap the attachment's button.

The attached file opens in the Viewer app.

**Note:** The Viewer app provides basic features for viewing widely used document types, such as PDF files, Microsoft Word documents, and Microsoft Excel workbooks. If the Viewer app cannot open the file you try to open, your iPod touch tries to suggest a suitable app.

**7** Tap **Open Attachment** ().

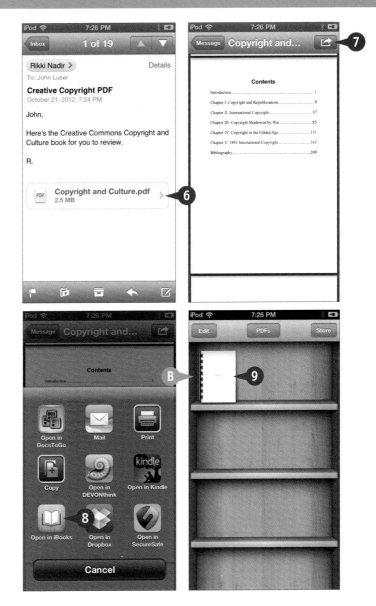

A screen for opening or using the attachment appears.

**8** Tap the app in which you want to open the document. For example, tap **Open in iBooks**.

**Ⓑ** The file opens in the app you chose.

**9** Depending on the app, tap the file to open it.

**Note:** After you open an attached file in an app, your iPod touch stores a copy of the file in that app's storage. You can then open the file again directly from that app.

---

**TIP**

**How can I delete an attached file from an e-mail message?**
You cannot directly delete an attached file from an e-mail message on the iPod touch at this writing. You can delete only the message along with its attached file. If you use an e-mail app such as Apple Mail to manage the same e-mail account, you can remove the attached file using that app. When you update your mailbox on your iPod touch, the iPod touch deletes the attached file but leaves the message.

# Search for E-Mail Messages

To find a particular e-mail message, you can open the inbox for the account that contains it and then browse for the message. But often you can locate a message more quickly by searching for it using a name or keyword that you know appears in the message's From field, To field, or Subject field. You cannot search the bodies of messages at this writing.

You can search either in a single inbox or in all your inboxes at once. Searching all inboxes is useful when you are not sure which e-mail account contains the message.

## Search for E-Mail Messages

1 Press the Home button.

The Home screen appears.

2 Tap **Mail**.

The Mailboxes screen appears.

3 Tap the inbox you want to open.

A Tap **All Inboxes** if you want to search all your inboxes for the message.

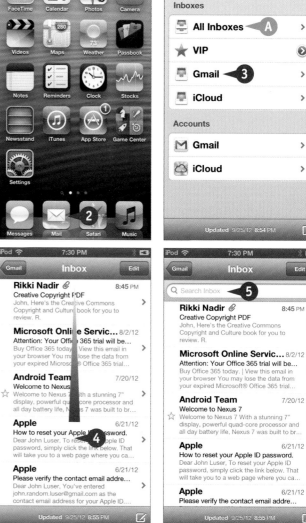

The inbox opens.

4 Tap and drag down to scroll up to the top of the screen.

**Note:** You can also tap the bar at the top of the screen to scroll to the top far enough to reveal the Search box.

The Search box appears.

5 Tap **Search Inboxes**.

The Search screen appears.

**6** Tap the message part you want to search in: From, To, Subject, or All. This example uses Subject.

**7** Tap in the Search box, and type your search term.

A list of search results appears.

**8** Tap the message you want to open.

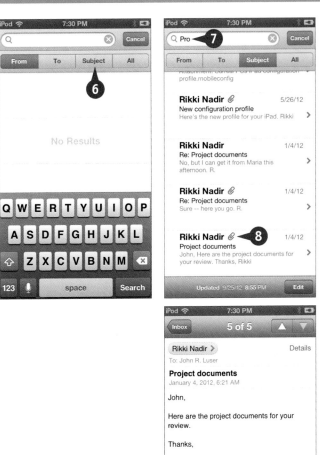

The message opens.

**Is there another way to search for e-mail messages?**

Yes. You can use the iPod touch's general search functionality to return e-mail matches along with other search results. Press the Home button to display the Home screen, and then press again to display the Search screen. Type your search term, locate the Mail search results, and then tap the message you want to see.

# CHAPTER 9

# Working with Contacts and Calendars

To stay organized, your iPod touch can manage your contacts, keep your schedule, track commitments, and carry important documents.

# Browse or Search for Contacts

To see which contacts you have synced to your iPod touch, or to find a particular contact, you can browse through the contacts.

You can either browse through your full list of contacts or choose to display only particular groups — for example, you can display only your business-related contacts by selecting the appropriate group. You can also search for contacts to locate them.

## Browse or Search for Contacts

### Browse Your Contacts

**1** Press the Home button.

The Home screen appears.

**2** Tap **Utilities**.

The Utilities folder opens.

**3** Tap **Contacts**.

The Contacts screen appears.

**A** To navigate the screen of contacts quickly, tap the letter on the right that you want to jump to. To navigate more slowly, scroll up or down.

**4** Tap the contact whose information you want to view.

The contact's screen appears.

**5** If necessary, tap and drag up to scroll down the screen to display more information.

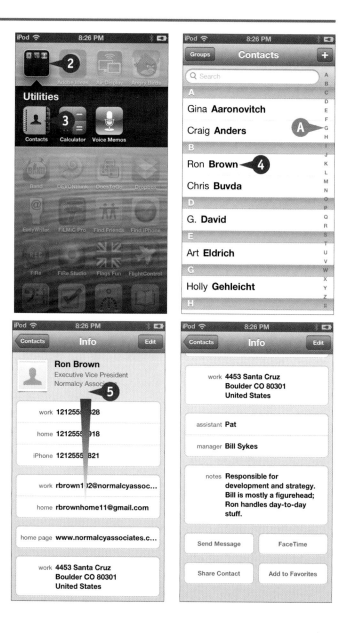

## Choose Which Groups of Contacts to Display

**1** From the Contacts list, tap **Groups**.

**2** On the Groups screen, tap **Show All Contacts**.

Contacts displays a check mark next to each group.

**Note:** When you tap **Show All Contacts**, the Hide All Contacts button appears in place of the Show All Contacts button. You can tap **Hide All Contacts** to remove all the check marks.

**3** Tap a group to apply a check mark to it or to remove the existing check mark.

**4** Tap **Done**.

The Contacts list appears, showing the contacts in the groups you selected.

## Search for Contacts

**1** From the Contacts list, tap **Search**.

**2** On the Search screen, type the name you want to search for.

**3** From the list of matches, tap the contact you want to view.

The contact's information appears.

**How do I make my iPod touch sort my contacts by last names instead of first names?**

Press the Home button. Tap **Settings** and then **Mail, Contacts, Calendars**. In the Contacts box, tap **Sort Order**. Tap **Last, First**.

**What does "Unified Info" mean at the top of a contact record?**

Unified Info means that Contacts is displaying information drawn from two or more contact records for the same contact. Look at the Linked Contacts area of the screen to see which contact records are providing the information.

# Create a New Contact

Normally, you put contacts on your iPod touch by syncing them from existing records on your computer or on an online service such as iCloud. But when necessary, you can create a new contact on your iPod touch itself — for example, when you meet someone you want to remember.

You can then sync the contact record back to your computer, adding the new contact to your existing contacts.

## Create a New Contact

**1** Press the Home button.

The Home screen appears.

**2** Tap **Utilities**.

The Utilities folder opens.

**3** Tap **Contacts**.

The Contacts screen appears.

**4** Tap **Add** (⊞).

The New Contact screen appears.

**5** Tap **First**.

The on-screen keyboard appears.

**6** Type the first name.

**7** Tap **Last**.

**8** Type the last name.

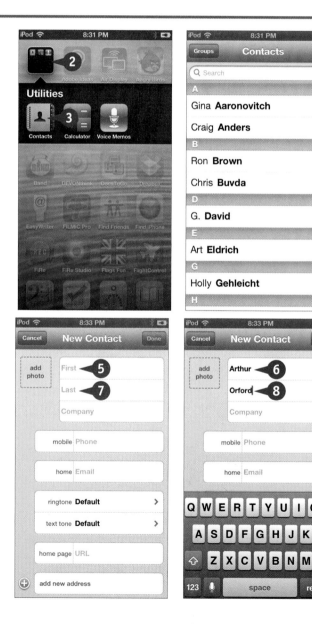

**9** Add other information as needed by tapping each field and then typing the information.

**10** To add a photo of the contact, tap **add photo**.

The Photo dialog opens.

**11** Tap **Take Photo**.

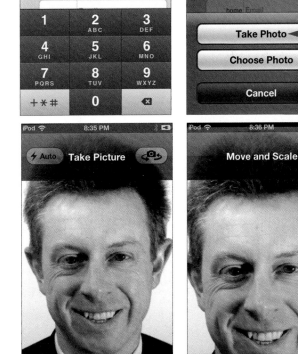

The Take Picture screen appears.

**12** Compose the photo, and then tap **Take Picture** (◉).

The Move and Scale screen appears.

**13** Position the part of the photo you want to use in the middle.

**Note:** Pinch in with two fingers to zoom the photo out. Pinch out with two fingers to zoom the photo in.

**14** Tap **Use Photo**.

The photo appears in the contact record.

**15** Tap **Done**.

**How do I assign my new contact an existing photo?**

**1** In the Photo dialog, tap **Choose Photo**.

**2** On the Photos screen, tap the photo album.

**3** Tap the photo.

**4** On the Move and Scale screen, position the photo, and then tap **Choose**.

# Share Contacts via E-Mail and Text Messages

Often in business or your personal life, you will need to share your contacts with other people. Your iPod touch makes it easy to share a contact record either via e-mail or via Apple's Messages service.

The iPod touch shares the contact record as a virtual business card in the widely used vCard format. Most phones and personal-organizer software can easily import vCard files.

## Share Contacts via E-Mail and Text Messages

### Open the Contact You Want to Share

**1** Press the Home button.

The Home screen appears.

**2** Tap **Utilities**.

The Utilities folder opens.

**3** Tap **Contacts**.

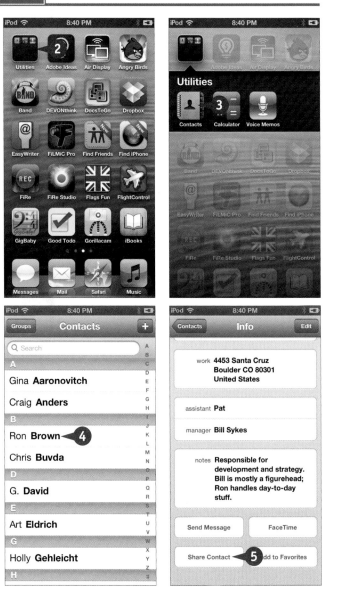

The Contacts screen appears.

**4** Tap the contact you want to share.

The Info screen for the contact appears.

**5** Tap **Share Contact**.

The Share Contact Using dialog opens.

## Share a Contact via E-Mail

**1** In the Share Contact Using dialog, tap **Email**.

**A** A new message titled Contact appears in the Mail app, with the contact record attached as a vCard file.

**2** Address the message by typing the address or by tapping ⊕ and choosing a contact as the recipient.

**3** Type a subject.

**4** Type a message.

**5** Tap **Send**, and Mail sends the message with the contact record attached.

## Share a Contact via Text Message

**1** In the Share Contact Using dialog, tap **Message**.

**B** The New Message screen appears, with the contact record attached to the message.

**2** Address the message by typing the name or number or by tapping ⊕ and choosing a contact as the recipient.

**3** Type a message.

**4** Tap **Send**, and the iPod touch sends the message with the contact record attached.

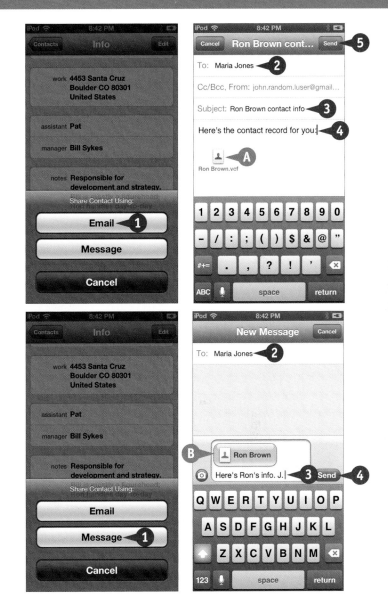

---

**TIP**

**How do I add a vCard I receive in an e-mail message to my contacts?**

In the Mail app, tap the button for the vCard file. On the vCard screen that opens, scroll down to the bottom, and then tap **Create New Contact**. If the vCard contains extra information about an existing contact, tap **Add to Existing Contact**, and then tap the contact.

Your iPod touch's Calendar app gives you a great way of managing your schedule and making sure you never miss an appointment.

After setting up your calendars to sync using iTunes, iCloud, or another calendar service, as described in Chapter 2, you can take your calendars with you everywhere and consult them whenever you need to. You can view either all your calendars or only ones you choose.

## Browse Existing Events in Your Calendars

### Browse Existing Events in Your Calendars

 **1** Press the Home button.

The Home screen appears.

**2** Tap **Calendar**.

The Calendar screen appears. Normally, you see the All Calendars screen.

**3** Tap **Month** to see Month view, in which each day appears in a square.

**Note:** In Month view, a dot on a date indicates that one or more events occur on that day.

**4** Tap the day you want to view.

**A** The day's details appear below the list of days.

**5** Tap **Day**.

A timeline with events for the current day appears.

**6** Tap **List**.

A list of upcoming appointments appears.

**7** Tap an appointment whose details you want to see.

The Event Details screen appears, showing details of the event.

**8** If you need to edit the event, tap **Edit**.

The Edit screen appears, and you can make changes to the event.

**9** Tap **Done**.

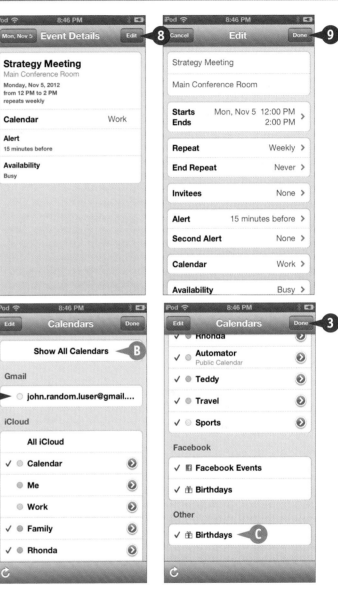

## Choose Which Calendars to Display

**1** Tap **Calendars**.

The Calendars screen appears.

**2** Tap to place a check mark next to a calendar you want to display, or tap to remove the check mark from a calendar you want to hide.

**Ⓑ** Tap **Show All Calendars** to place a check mark next to each calendar. Tap **Hide All Calendars** to remove all check marks.

**Ⓒ** The Birthdays calendar automatically displays birthdays of contacts whose contact data includes the birthday.

**3** When you finish choosing calendars to display, tap **Done**.

The calendars you chose appear.

**TIP**

**How can I quickly find an event?**
In the Calendar app, tap **List** to display the List screen, and then tap **Search** ( 🔍 ). Type your search term. When Calendar displays a list of matches, tap the event you want to view.

Normally, you will probably create most new events in your calendars on your computer, and then sync them to your iPod touch. But when you need to create a new event using the iPod touch, you can easily do so.

You can create either a straightforward, one-shot appointment or an appointment that repeats on a schedule. And you can choose which calendar the appointment belongs to.

## Create New Events in Your Calendars

**1** Press the Home button.

The Home screen appears.

**2** Tap **Calendar**.

The Calendar screen appears.

**3** Tap **Month** to switch to Month view.

**4** Tap the day on which you want to create the new event.

**5** Tap **Add** (➕).

The Add Event screen appears.

**6** Tap **Title** and type the title of the event.

**7** Tap **Location** and type the location of the event.

**8** Tap **Starts, Ends**.

The Start & End screen appears.

**9** Tap the date and time wheels to set the start time.

**10** Tap **Ends**.

**11** Tap the date and time wheels to set the end time.

**A** If this is an all-day appointment, tap the **All-day** switch and move it to On.

**B** If you need to change the time zone, tap **Time Zone**, type the city name, and then tap the time zone.

**12** Tap **Done**.

**13** On the Add Event screen, tap **Alert**.

**14** On the Event Alert screen, tap the timing for the alert.

**15** Tap **Done**.

**16** Tap **Calendar**.

**17** On the Calendar screen, tap the calendar for the event.

**18** Tap **Done**.

**19** On the Add Event screen, tap **Done**.

The event appears on your calendar.

## TIP

**How do I set up an event that repeats every week?**

On the Add Event screen, tap **Repeat**. On the Repeat screen, tap **Every Week** (**A**), placing a check mark next to it, and then tap **Done**.

# Work with Calendar Invitations

As well as events you create yourself, you may receive invitations to events that others create. When you receive an event invitation attached to an e-mail message, you can choose whether to accept the invitation or decline it. If you accept the invitation, you can add the event automatically to your calendar.

## Work with Calendar Invitations

### Deal with an Invitation from an Alert

1. When an invitation alert appears, tap **View**.

2. On the Event Details screen, tap **Calendar**, if you decide to accept the invitation.

3. On the Calendar screen, tap the Calendar to which you want to assign the event.

Ⓐ A check mark appears next to the calendar.

4. Tap the event's name.

5. On the Event Details screen, tap **Alert**, if you want to set an alert to remind yourself about the event.

6. On the Event Alert screen, tap the button for the alert interval. For example, tap **1 hour before**.

Ⓑ A check mark appears on the button.

7. Tap the event's name.

8. On the Event Details screen, tap **Availability**, if you need to change whether the time appears in your calendar as Busy or Free.

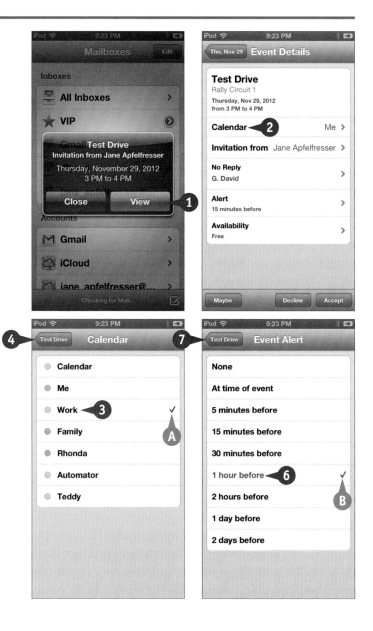

156

**9** On the Availability screen, tap **Busy** or **Free**, as appropriate.

**C** A check mark appears on the button you tapped.

**10** Tap the event's name.

**11** On the Event Details screen, tap the date button in the upper left corner.

**D** Your calendar appears, showing the event you accepted.

## Deal with an Invitation from the Invitations Screen

**E** In your calendar, the Invitations button shows an alert giving the number of invitations.

**1** Tap **Invitations** ().

**2** On the Invitations screen, tap **Accept**, **Decline**, or **Maybe**, as needed.

**Note:** To see the full detail of the invitation, tap its button on the Invitations screen. The Event Details screen then appears, and you can accept the invitation as described earlier in this task.

**3** Tap **Done**.

**Why does an event appear at a different time than that shown in the invitation I accepted?**
When you open the invitation, you see the event's time in the time zone in which it was created. If your iPod touch is currently using a different time zone, the appointment appears in your calendar using that time zone's time, so the time appears to have changed.

# Keep Track of Your Commitments with Reminders

Your iPod touch's Reminders app gives you an easy way to note your commitments and keep track of them.

You can create a reminder with no due time or location, but to get the most out of the Reminders app, you should tie each reminder to a due time. When you create such reminders, your iPod touch can remind you of them at the appropriate time.

## Keep Track of Your Commitments with Reminders

### Open the Reminders App

 Press the Home button.

The Home screen appears.

 Tap **Reminders**.

The Reminders screen appears.

**Note:** When you complete a task, tap ☐ to the left of the reminder (☐ changes to ☑).

### Create a New Reminder

 In the Reminders app, tap ✛.

Reminders starts a new reminder beneath the last reminder, and displays the on-screen keyboard.

 Type the text of the reminder.

 Tap the **return** button.

**Note:** To create a reminder using Siri, press the Home button for a couple of seconds until Siri bleeps, and then say the reminder aloud. For example, say "Remind me at 8 a.m. tomorrow to take the project files to the office," or say "Remember to talk to Bill about the magazine when I get to the office today."

The new reminder appears in the list.

4 Tap the button for the new reminder.

The Details screen appears.

5 Tap the **Remind Me On a Day** switch and move it to the On position.

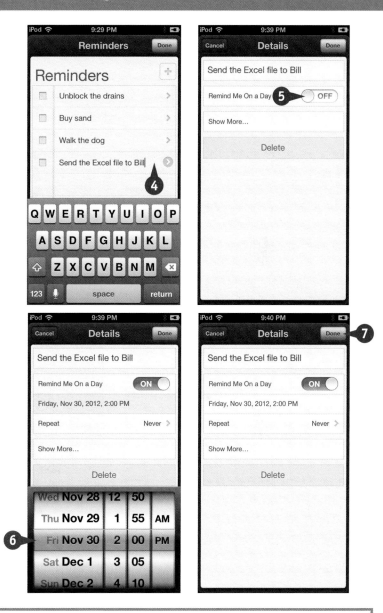

Date and time spin wheels appear.

6 Select the date and time for the reminder.

7 Tap **Done**.

TIP

**How do I sync my iPod touch's reminders with my Mac's reminders?**

You can sync your iPod touch's reminders with your Mac's reminders via your iCloud account.

On your iPod touch, press the Home button to display the Home screen, and then tap **Settings** to display the Settings screen. Tap **iCloud** to display the iCloud screen, and then move the **Reminders** switch to the On position.

On your Mac, click  and **System Preferences** to open System Preferences. Click **iCloud** to display the iCloud pane, and then select the **Calendars & Reminders** check box ( changes to ☑).

You can organize your reminders into different lists, so that you can look at a single category of reminders at a time. For example, you may find it useful to create a Work list that enables you to focus on your work-related reminders.

After creating lists, you can easily switch among them. You can also move a reminder from one list to another as needed. And when you no longer need a particular reminder, you can delete it.

**Keep Track of Your Commitments with Reminders** (continued)

### Create Different Lists of Reminders

**1** From the Reminders screen, tap ☰.

The Lists screen appears.

**2** Tap **Edit**.

**3** Tap **Create New List**.

**4** Type the name for the new list.

**5** Tap **Done**. The Reminders app adds the new list to the Lists screen.

Reminders displays the Reminders screen again.

### Switch among Your Reminders Lists

**1** From the Reminders screen, tap ☰.

The Lists screen appears.

**2** Tap the list you want to display.

The list appears.

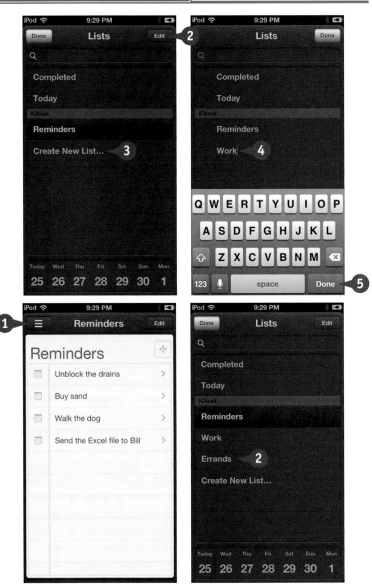

## Change the List to Which a Reminder Is Assigned

**1** From a Reminders list, tap the reminder.

**2** On the Details screen, tap **Show More**.

**3** Tap **List**.

**4** On the List screen, tap the list to which you want to assign the reminder.

**5** Tap **Done**.

**6** On the Details screen, tap **Done**.

## Delete a Reminder

**1** From a Reminders list, tap **Edit**.

The list switches to Edit mode.

**Note:** Normally, you remove a reminder from your Reminders list by marking it as complete. Delete a reminder only when you do not need to complete it.

**2** Tap ⊖ to the left of the reminder you want to delete.

**3** Tap **Delete**.

Reminders deletes the reminder.

**Note:** You can also delete a reminder by tapping **Delete** on its Details screen, and then tapping **Delete** in the confirmation dialog that appears.

**4** Tap **Done**.

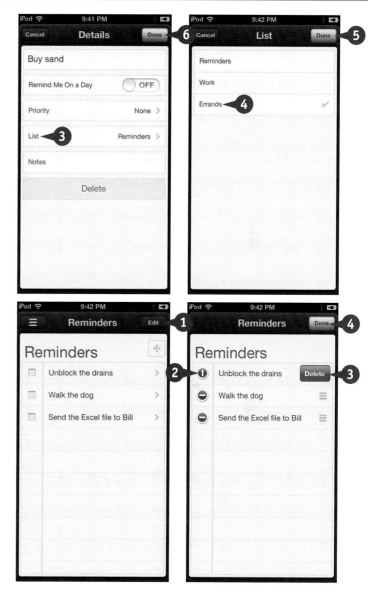

## TIP

**Can I change the default list that Reminders puts my reminders in?**
Yes, you can change the default list in the Settings app. Press the Home button to display the Home screen, and then tap **Settings** to display the Settings screen. Tap **Reminders** to display the Reminders screen, tap **Default List** to display the Default List screen, and then tap the list you want to make the default. On the Reminders screen, you can also choose how many reminders to sync — **2 Weeks**, **1 Month**, **3 Months**, **6 Months**, or **All Reminders**.

# Keep Essential Documents at Hand with Passbook

Passbook is an app for storing electronic versions of essential documents such as boarding passes, cinema tickets, and hotel reservations.

To get your documents into Passbook, you use apps such as Mail and Safari. For example, when an airline sends you your travel details attached to an e-mail message, you can add the boarding pass to Passbook from Mail. You can also add documents using custom apps for shopping, booking hotels, and booking flights.

## Keep Essential Documents at Hand with Passbook

### Add a Document to Passbook

 In Mail, tap the message with the document attached.

The message opens.

**2** Tap the document's button.

The document appears.

**3** Tap **Add**.

Mail adds the document to Passbook.

The message appears again.

**Note:** In Safari, open the web page containing the document, and then tap **Add** to add it to Passbook.

### Open Passbook and Find the Documents You Need

**1** Press the Home button.

The Home screen appears.

**2** Tap **Passbook**.

Passbook opens.

The documents you have added appear.

**Note:** Until you add one or more documents to Passbook, the app displays an information screen highlighting its uses.

 Tap the document you want to view.

**A** The document appears above the other documents. You can then hold its barcode in front of a scanner to use the document.

**4** When you need to see another document, tap the current top document and drag down.

**5** At the bottom of the screen, release the document.

Passbook reshuffles the documents so you can see them all.

## Choose Settings for a Document or Delete It

**1** Tap 🛈.

The document rotates so you can see its back.

**2** Tap the **Notifications** switch and set it to On if you want to receive notifications about updates to this document.

**3** Tap the **Show On Lock Screen** switch and set it to On if you want notifications to appear on the lock screen.

**B** If you have no further need for the document, tap 🗑 to delete the document.

**4** When you finish reviewing the document's details, tap **Done**.

The document rotates again to display its front.

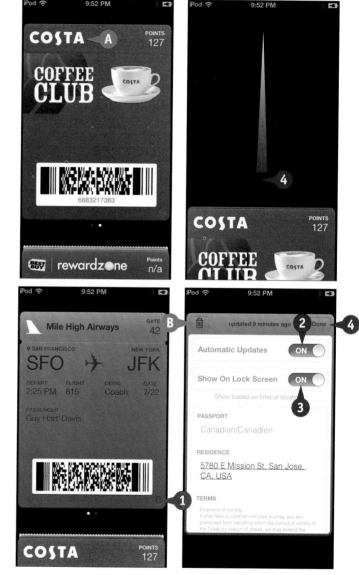

## TIP

**How do Mail and Safari know which documents belong in Passbook and which do not?**
Passbook documents use a special file format and internal file structure that tell apps such as Mail and Safari to treat them as Passbook items. Mail and Safari will not add "normal" documents — for example, Word documents — to Passbook.

# CHAPTER 10

# Playing Music and Videos

As well as being a powerful handheld computer and digital camera, your iPod touch is also a full-scale music and video player. To play music, you use the Music app; to play videos, you use the Videos app. In this chapter, you learn to use the Music app to play back music and create playlists. You also learn how to enjoy podcasts and iTunes U lectures, play videos, and shop on the iTunes Store.

# Play Back Music Using the Music App

fter loading music on your iPod touch as described in the task "Choose Which Items to Sync" in Chapter 1, you can play it back using the Music app.

You can play music in several ways. You can play music by song or by album, as described in this task. You can play songs in exactly the order you want by creating a custom playlist, as described later in this chapter. You can also play by artist, by genre, or by composer.

## Play Back Music Using the Music App

**1** Press the Home button.

The Home screen appears.

**2** Tap **Music**.

The Music screen appears.

**3** Tap the button by which you want to sort. This example uses **Songs**.

The list of songs appears.

**A** To see the music listed by other categories, such as Composers or Genres, tap **More**, and then tap the category by which you want to sort.

**4** Tap and drag up to scroll down the screen, if necessary.

**5** Tap the song you want to play.

**Note:** Tap and hold for a moment to see the full information about the song — for example, if it does not fit in the listing.

The song starts playing.

**6** Tap and drag the slider to change the position in the song.

**7** Tap  once to turn on repeating (⟳), again to repeat only the current song (⟳), and a third time to turn off repeating (⟳).

**8** Tap ⤬ to turn on shuffling (⤬). Tap again to turn off shuffling (⤬).

**9** Tap ✳ to create a Genius automatic playlist based on this song.

**10** To rate the song or jump to another song, tap **Song List** (☰).

The song list appears.

**11** Tap the appropriate star to rate the song.

**12** Tap another song to play it, or tap **Song** to go back to the song.

---

**TIP**

**Is there a way to control the Music app's playback when I have switched to another app?**

Yes. You can quickly control the Music app using the app-switching bar. Press the Home button twice in quick succession to display the app-switching bar, and then scroll left until you see the

playback controls. Tap **Pause** (⏸) to pause the music, and tap **Play** (▶) to restart playback. Tap **Fast-Forward/Next** (⏭) to skip to the next track, or tap and hold to fast-forward. Tap **Rewind/Previous** (⏮) to go back to the beginning of the track, tap again to go to the previous track, or tap and hold to rewind. Tap **Music** (♪) to display the Music app.

# Play Back Videos Using the Videos App

To play videos — such as movies, TV shows, or music videos — you use the iPod touch's Videos app. You can play back a video either on the iPod touch's screen, which is handy when you are traveling, or on a TV to which you connect the iPod touch, or to a TV connected to an Apple TV box. Using a TV is great when you need to share a movie or other video with family, friends, or colleagues.

## Play Back Videos Using the Videos App

**1** Press the Home button.

The Home screen appears.

**Note:** You can also play videos that are included on web pages. To do so, press Home, tap **Safari**, navigate to the page, and then tap the video.

**2** Tap **Videos**.

The Videos screen appears.

**Note:** Tap and drag up to scroll down the screen to see more videos.

**3** Tap the video you want to play.

**Note:** Your iPod touch plays video in the orientation it was shot or produced — typically landscape orientation. So if you are holding the iPod touch in its upright, portrait orientation, turn it on its side for viewing the video.

The video starts playing.

**4** When you need to control playback, tap the screen.

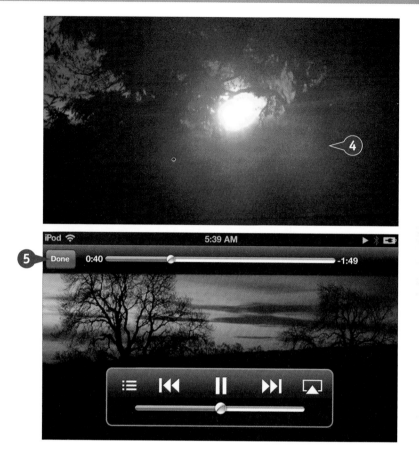

The playback controls appear, and you can pause the video, move forward, or take other actions.

**5** Tap **Done** when you want to stop playing the video.

---

### TIP

**How do I play back videos on my television from my iPod touch?**

First, check which connectors the television uses, and then get a suitable connector cable from the Apple Store (http://store.apple.com) or another supplier. For example, you may need the Apple Composite AV Cable or an equivalent for a standard TV. If possible, use a component connection for a standard TV, and use an HDMI connection for an HDTV.

Second, use the cable to connect the iPod touch's Lightning port to the television.

Third, tap **Settings**, tap **General**, and then tap **TV Out** to display the TV Out screen. Tap the **Widescreen** switch and move it to On or Off, as needed. To change the TV output, tap **TV Signal**, and then tap **NTSC** or **PAL**, as needed.

# Create a Playlist with the Music App

Instead of playing individual songs or playing a CD's songs from start to finish, you can create a playlist that contains only the songs you want in your preferred order. Playlists are a great way to enjoy music on your iPod touch.

You can create either a standard playlist by putting the songs in order yourself, or use the Genius Playlist feature to have the Music app create the playlist for you. Before you can use the Genius Playlist feature, you must turn on Genius in iTunes and then sync your iPod touch.

## Create a Playlist with the Music App

**1** Press the Home button.

The Home screen appears.

**2** Tap **Music**.

The Music screen appears.

**3** Tap **Playlists**.

The Playlists screen appears.

**Ⓐ** The Genius symbol (※) indicates a Genius playlist.

**4** Tap **Add Playlist**.

The New Playlist dialog opens.

**5** Type the name for the playlist.

**6** Tap **Save**.

The Songs screen appears.

**7** Tap ⊕ for each song you want to add, or simply tap the song's button.

**B** The song button fades to gray to show you have added the song to the playlist.

**C** To browse by artists for songs to add, tap **Artists**. To browse by playlists, tap **Playlists**. To browse by albums, tap **Albums**.

**8** Tap **Done**.

The playlist screen appears.

**9** Tap **Edit**.

The screen for editing the playlist appears.

**10** Tap ≡ and drag a song up or down to move it.

**D** To remove a song, tap ⊖.

**E** To add further songs, tap ＋.

**11** Tap **Done** at the top of the playlist editing screen.

**12** Tap a song to start the playlist playing.

**F** Tap **Shuffle** if you want to play the playlist's songs in random order.

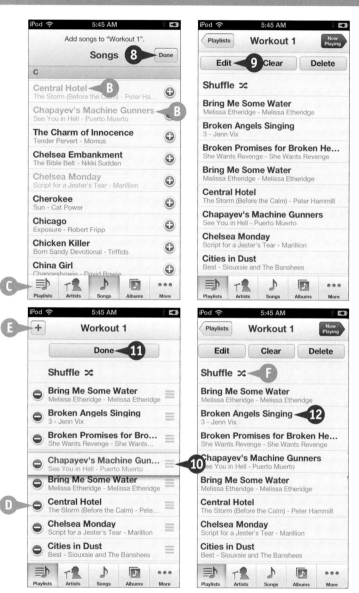

**How do I create a Genius playlist on my iPod touch?**

Press the Home button. Tap **Music**, tap **Playlists**, and then tap **Genius Playlist**. Tap the song to base the playlist on (**A**). The Music app creates the playlist and sets it playing.

# Customize the Music App's Interface

The Music app comes set up so that you can easily browse by playlists, artists, songs, or albums. If you want to browse by other categories, such as by composers or by genres, you can customize the Music app's interface to put these items at the tip of your finger.

## Customize the Music App's Interface

**1** Press the Home button.

The Home screen appears.

**2** Tap **Music**.

The Music screen appears.

**3** Tap **More**.

The More screen appears.

**4** Tap **Edit**.

The Configure screen appears.

**5** Tap a button and drag it to replace a button on the button bar. For example, tap **Genres** and drag it on top of **Albums**.

The button you dropped replaces the button you dropped it on.

**6** Change other buttons as needed.

**Note:** You can change the position of the buttons on the button bar by tapping a button and dragging it left or right to where you want it.

**7** Tap **Done**.

**A** You can then use your customized version of the Music screen.

---

**TIP**

**How do I reset the Music screen to its default settings?**
The straightforward way to reset the Music app's screen to its default settings is to display the Configure screen as described in this task, and drag the icons into their default order: Playlists, Artists, Songs, Albums, and More.

You can also return the Music app's screen to its default configuration from the Reset screen in Settings, but this is a wide-ranging change that you normally do not want to make.

# Use Podcasts and iTunes U

esides listening to music and watching videos, you can use your iPod touch to watch or listen to *podcasts*, which are video or audio programs released via the Internet.

You can find podcasts covering many different topics by using Apple's Podcasts app. Similarly, you can use the iTunes U app to access podcasts containing free educational content.

## Use Podcasts and iTunes U

① Press the Home button.

The Home screen appears.

② Tap **Podcasts**.

**Note:** If the Podcasts app does not appear on the Home screen, go to the App Store and install it. See Chapter 7 for instructions on installing apps.

The Podcasts app opens.

**Note:** At first, when you have added no podcasts, you see an informational message.

③ Tap **Catalog**.

④ Tap **Categories**.

The Categories screen appears.

⑤ Tap the category you want to see.

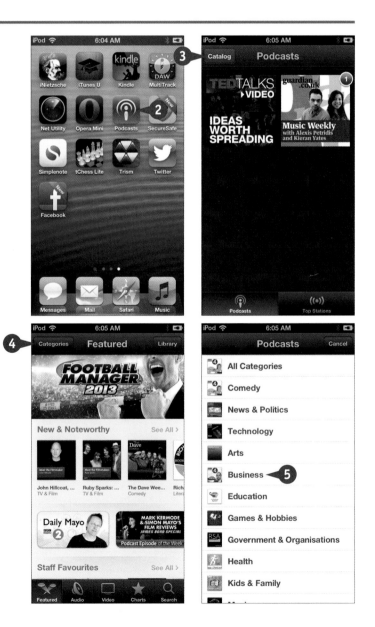

Tap **Featured**, **Audio**, **Video**, or **Charts**, as needed.

**Note:** You can also search for podcasts by tapping **Search** and then typing search terms in the Search box.

 Tap the podcast you want to view.

⑧ Tap **Subscribe** if you want to subscribe to the podcast.

⑨ Tap ⬇ to download an episode of the podcast.

⑩ Tap the button in the upper left corner to display the previous screen.

⑪ Tap **Library**.

⑫ Tap the podcast whose episodes you want to see.

⑬ Tap the episode you want to play.

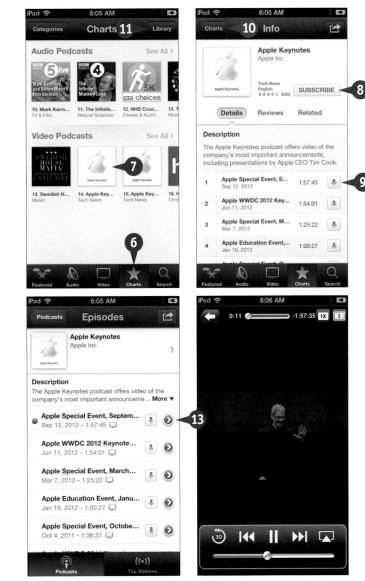

**How do I use iTunes U?**

iTunes U works in a similar way to the Podcasts app. Press the Home button, and then tap **iTunes U** to launch the app. Tap **Catalog** to display the Catalog screen, and then browse to find lectures you want to view. Tap **Library** to display the Library screen, and then tap the item you want to play.

# Shop for Music and Video at the iTunes Store

To find music and videos for your iPod touch, you can shop at Apple's iTunes Store by using the iTunes app.

When you buy music or videos from the iTunes Store using the iTunes app, the iPod touch downloads the files, so you can play them immediately. When you sync your iPod touch with your computer, iTunes copies the music or videos you have bought to your computer. If you use your iPod touch without a computer, you can sync the files to iCloud so that you can use them on your other devices — for example, on an iPad.

## Shop for Music and Video at the iTunes Store

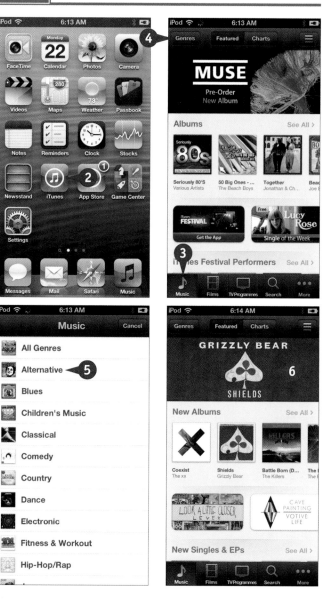

1. Press the Home button.

   The Home screen appears.

2. Tap **iTunes**.

   The iTunes screen appears.

3. Tap **Music** or **Videos** on the button bar to display the type of content you want. This example uses **Music**.

   The screen you chose appears.

4. Tap **Genres**.

   The Genres screen appears.

5. Tap the genre you want to display — for example, **Alternative**.

   The genre's screen appears.

6. Tap the album or song you want to display.

The album's screen appears.

**7** Tap a song title to play a preview.

**Ⓐ** Tap **Stop** (◼) to stop the preview playing.

**8** To buy a song, tap the price button.

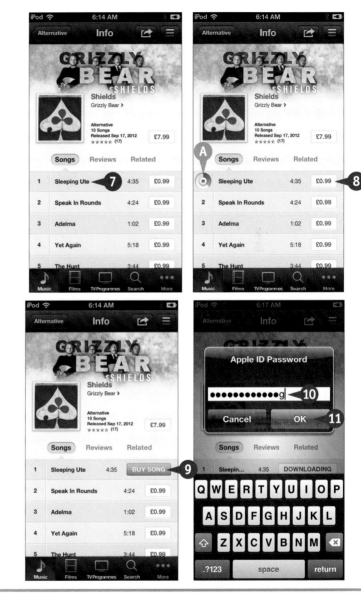

The Buy Song button replaces the price button.

**9** Tap **Buy Song**.

The Apple ID Password dialog opens.

**10** Type your password.

**11** Tap **OK**.

iTunes downloads the song, and you can play it using the Music app.

---

**TIP**

**How can I find the music I want at the iTunes Store?**

You can easily search for music within the iTunes app. Tap **Search** on the button bar at the bottom of the screen, and then type a search term (Ⓐ). iTunes shows matching results as you type. Tap the result you want to view.

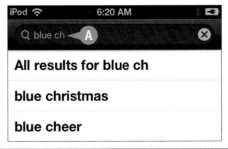

# CHAPTER 11

# Working with Photos and Books

In this chapter, you learn to use your iPod touch's Photos app to view photos. You also learn to use the iBooks app to read e-books and PDF files.

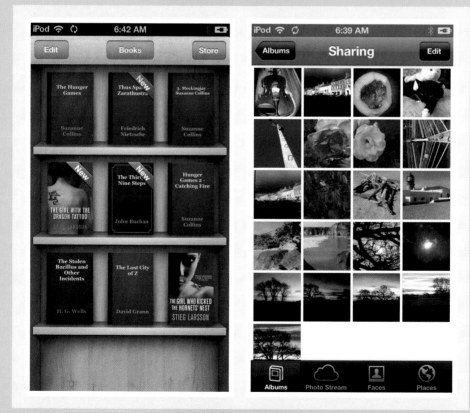

Y ou can use the Photos app to browse the photos you have taken with your iPod touch's camera, photos you have synced using iTunes or via your Photo Stream on iCloud, and photos you receive in e-mail messages or download from web pages.

The most straightforward way to browse is by albums, but you can also browse by events, faces, and places. An *event* is a named collection of photos associated with a particular date or happening; a *face* is a person's face you teach iPhoto to recognize; and a *place* is a geographical location.

## Browse Your Photos Using Events, Faces, and Places

### Open the Photos App and Browse by Albums

 Press the Home button.

The Home screen appears.

 Tap **Photos**.

The Photos app opens.

**3** Tap **Albums**.

The Albums screen appears.

**4** Tap the album you want to view. In this example, the album is named Sharing.

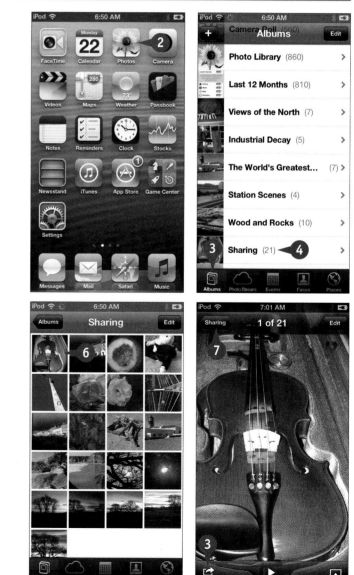

The album's screen appears.

**Note:** The Camera Roll album contains the photos you have taken using the iPod touch's camera.

**5** Tap and drag up to scroll down the screen through the photos.

**6** Tap the photo you want to view.

The photo appears.

**Note:** Swipe your finger to the left to display the next photo, or swipe to the right to display the previous photo.

**7** Tap the button with the album's name to return to the album's screen.

## Browse by Events

 **1** In the Photos app, tap **Events**.

The list of events appears.

 **2** Tap the event you want to view.

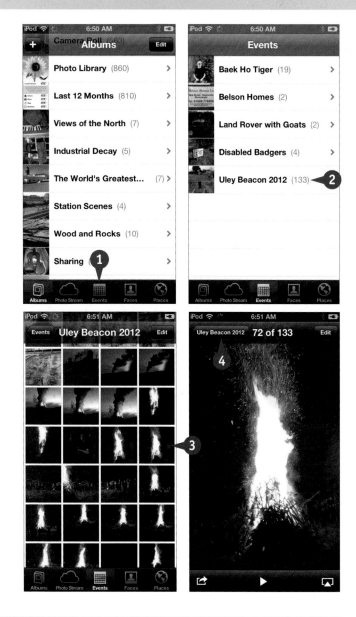

The photos in the event appear.

 **3** Tap the photo you want to see.

The photo appears.

**Note:** Swipe your finger to the left to display the next photo, or swipe to the right to display the previous photo.

 **4** Tap the event name when you want to return to the event.

TIP

**How can I move through a long list of photos more quickly?**
You can move through the photos more quickly by using momentum scrolling. Tap and flick up with your finger to set the photos scrolling. As the momentum drops, you can tap and flick up again to scroll further. Tap and drag your finger in the opposite direction to stop the scrolling.

continued ▶

If you allow the Camera app to access location information on your iPod touch, the Camera app automatically tags each photo with the location information for where you took it. You can then sort your photos by using the Places feature.

Being able to identify photos by location can be great for finding the photos you want. But it means that anybody you share the photos with knows exactly when and where you took them.

## Browse Your Photos Using Events, Faces, and Places (continued)

### Browse by Faces

1 In the Photos app, tap **Faces**.

The list of faces appears.

2 Tap the face you want to view.

The list of photos for the face appears.

3 Tap the photo you want to view.

The photo appears.

**Note:** Swipe your finger to the left to display the next photo, or swipe to the right to display the previous photo.

4 Tap the face's name button to return to the thumbnails of that individual's face.

5 Tap the **Faces** button to return to the Photo Library.

## Browse by Places

 In the Photos app, tap **Places**.

The Places map appears.

 Pinch out to zoom in on what you want to view.

**Note:** You can also zoom in by increments by double-tapping the target area of the screen.

 Tap the pinhead for the place you want to view.

The number of photos for the place appears.

 Tap ⊙ .

The photos in the place appear.

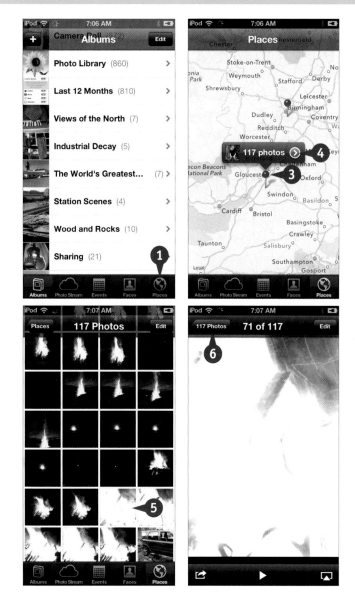 Tap the photo you want to view.

The photo appears.

**Note:** Swipe your finger to the left to display the next photo, or swipe to the right to display the previous photo.

 Tap **Photos** to return to the Photo Library.

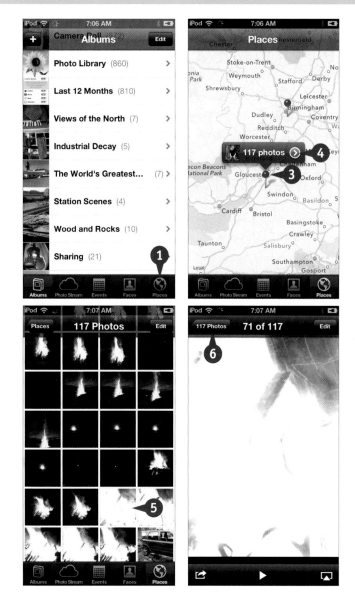

**Why does the Photos button bar not show a Faces button?**

The Faces button appears on the button bar in the Photos app only when you have synced photos with marked faces using iTunes. You must also have started using the Faces feature in iPhoto; if you have not, none of your photos will have marked faces. The iPod touch does not normally recognize Face information or Place information you assign in an image-editing application in Windows.

If you have an iCloud account, you can use the Photo Stream feature to share your photos among your iOS devices and your computer.

After you turn on Photo Stream on your iPod touch, other iOS devices, and your Macs, Photo Stream automatically syncs your 1,000 most recent photos among the devices and your computers.

## Share Your Photos with Your Computers and iOS Devices Using Photo Stream

### Turn On Photo Stream on Your iPod touch

**1** Press the Home button.

The Home screen appears.

**2** Tap **Settings**.

The Settings screen appears.

**3** Scroll down and then tap **iCloud**.

The iCloud screen appears.

**4** Tap **Photo Stream**.

The Photo Stream screen appears.

**5** Tap the **My Photo Stream** switch and move it to the On position.

**6** Tap **iCloud**.

The iCloud screen appears again.

## View Photo Stream on Your iPod touch

**1** Press the Home button.

The Home screen appears.

**2** Tap **Photos**.

The Photos screen appears, showing the previous screen you used — for example, the Albums screen.

**3** Tap **Photo Stream**.

The My Photo Stream screen appears.

**4** Tap the photo you want to view.

The photo opens.

## Share Photos from Photo Stream

**1** On the My Photo Stream screen, tap **Edit**.

The Select Photos screen appears.

**2** Tap each photo you want to select.

☑ appears on each photo you tap.

**3** Tap **Share**.

The Share screen appears.

**4** Tap the means of sharing. For example, tap **Mail** to share via e-mail.

**Note:** You can also delete photos from your photo stream. Select the photos as described here, and then tap **Delete**.

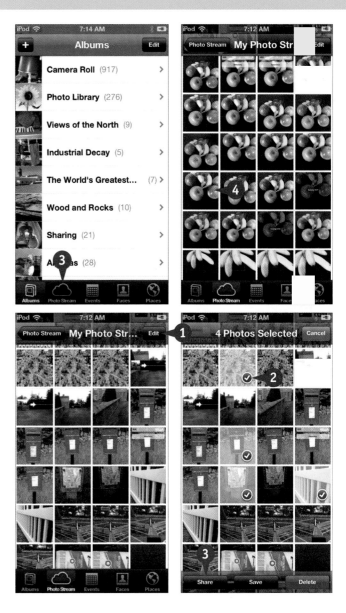

TIP

**How do I use Photo Stream on my computer?**

On a Mac, click  and **System Preferences**, and then click **iCloud** to display the iCloud pane. Click **Photo Stream** (☐ changes to ☑). Click **System Preferences** and **Quit System Preferences**. Next, click **iPhoto** (📷) on the Dock, and click **Photo Stream** in the Recent list in the Sidebar.

In Windows, click **Start** and **Control Panel**. Click **View By** and **Large Icons**, and then click **iCloud**. Click **Photo Stream** (☐ changes to ☑) and **Close**. Now click **Start** and **Computer**, navigate to the Photo Stream folder, and open it.

When you have set up Photo Stream on your iPod touch, other iOS devices, and Mac, you can not only share your photos among your computers but also share your photos with other people. Similarly, you can view the photo streams other people are sharing.

To share your Photo Stream, you turn on the Shared Photo Streams feature on your iPod touch. You can then create shared photo streams for specific people or groups of people.

## Share Photo Streams with Other People

### Turn On Shared Photo Streams

**1** Press the Home button.

The Home screen appears.

**2** Tap **Settings**.

The Settings screen appears.

**3** Scroll down and then tap **iCloud**.

The iCloud screen appears.

**4** Tap **Photo Stream**.

The Photo Stream screen appears.

**5** Tap the **Shared Photo Streams** switch and move it to the On position.

**6** Tap **iCloud**.

The iCloud screen appears again.

### Create a Shared Photo Stream

**1** Press the Home button.

The Home screen appears.

**2** Tap **Photos**.

The Photos screen appears, showing the previous screen you used — for example, the Albums screen.

**3** Tap **Photo Stream**.

The Photo Stream screen appears.

**4** Tap ➕.

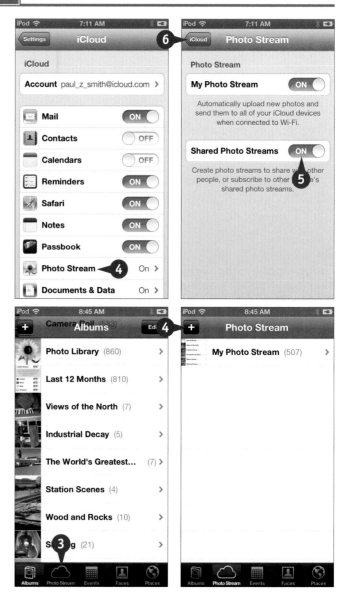

**5** Tap  to display the Contacts list, and then tap the contact with whom to share the photo stream.

**6** Tap **Name** and then type the name for the photo stream.

**7** Tap the **Public Website** switch and move it to the On position if you want to make the photo stream public.

**8** Tap **Create**.

**9** Tap the new photo stream on the Photo Stream screen.

The screen for the photo stream appears.

**10** Tap **Edit**.

The Select Items screen appears.

**11** Tap **Add**.

The Albums screen appears.

**12** Tap the source of photos you want to add. For example, tap an album.

The item opens.

**13** Tap each photo you want to add.

**14** Tap **Done**.

The photos appear in the photo stream.

**How do I view the Photo Streams other people are sharing?**

Turn on Shared Photo Streams as described in this task by moving the Shared Photo Streams switch on the Photo Stream screen to the On position. Next, when you receive an e-mail message prompting you to join a shared photo stream, tap **Join this Photo Stream**. Then, in Photos, tap **Photo Stream**, and then tap the shared photo stream's name.

From your iPod touch's Photos app, you can quickly share a photo either by sending it as an attachment to an e-mail message or by inserting it in an instant message.

## Share Photos via E-Mail and Messaging

### Select the Photo and Open the Share Dialog

1 Browse to the photo you want to share — see the preceding task.

2 Tap **Share** ( ).

The Share dialog opens. You can now share the photo as described in the steps that follow.

### Share the Photo via E-Mail

1 In the Share dialog, tap **Mail**.

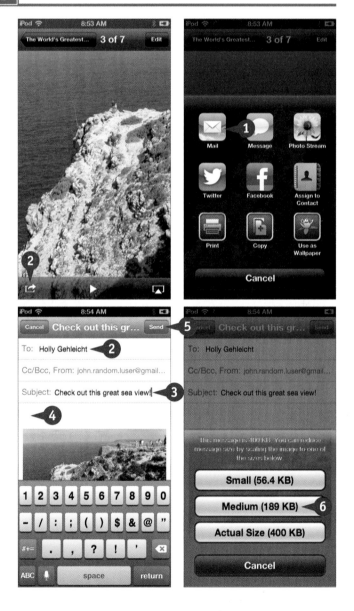

Your iPod touch creates a new e-mail message in the Mail app with the photo attached to the message.

2 Tap in the To box and address the e-mail message.

3 Tap in the Subject line and type the subject for the e-mail message.

4 Tap in the body area, and then type any text needed.

5 Tap **Send**.

6 If the Photos Size dialog opens, tap the button for the size of photo you want to send.

Mail sends the message.

## Share the Photo via Messaging

**1** In the Share dialog, tap **Message**.

Your iPod touch creates a new message in the Messages app with the photo attached to the message.

**2** Tap in the To box and address the message.

**3** Tap in the body area, and then type any text needed.

**4** Tap **Send**.

The Messages app sends the message.

## TIPS

**How do I send multiple photos at once via e-mail?**

From a screen that shows multiple photos, such as the Photo Library screen, tap **Share** (📷). The Select Photos screen appears. Tap each photo you want to send (Ⓐ), placing a check mark, up to a maximum of five photos. Then tap **Share** (Ⓑ), and then tap **Email** in the dialog that opens.

**What is the best size to use when sending photos via e-mail?**

This depends on what the recipient will do with the photo. If the recipient needs to edit or print the photo, choose **Actual Size**. If the recipient will merely view the photo on-screen, choose **Large** or **Medium**. The **Small** size works for contact card images, but its picture quality is too low for most other uses.

Your iPod touch can not only display your photos but also play them as a slide show. The slide show feature is limited to using existing groups of photos — you cannot create a slide show group on the iPod touch — but you can shuffle the photos into a different order. To make the most of your slide shows, you first choose the slide timing in the Photos screen in Settings. You can also choose to repeat the slide show or run the photos in random order. Then, when you start the slide show, you can choose which transition to use and add music.

## Play Slide Shows of Your Photos

1 Press the Home button.

2 On the Home screen, tap **Settings**.

3 On the Settings screen, tap **Photos & Camera**.

The Photos & Camera screen appears.

4 To make the slide show repeat, tap the **Repeat** switch and move it to On.

5 To play the photos in random order, tap the **Shuffle** switch and move it to On.

6 Tap **Play Each Slide For**.

7 Tap the appropriate button — for example, **5 Seconds**.

8 Tap **Photos & Camera**.

9 Press the Home button.

10 On the Home screen, tap **Photos**.

11 On the Photos screen, locate the photos for the slide show. For example, tap **Events**, and then tap the event.

12 When the photos appear, tap the photo at which you want to start the slide show.

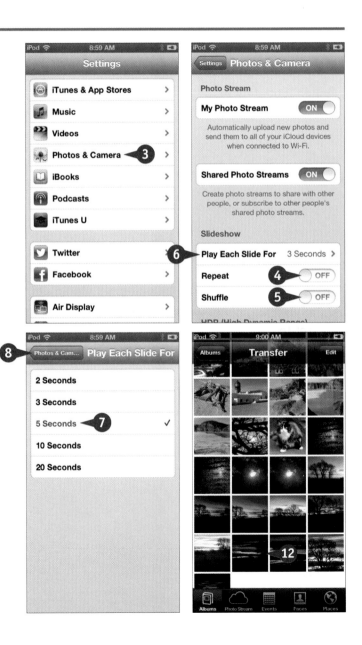

The photo appears.

 Tap **Start Slideshow** (▶).

The Slideshow Options screen appears.

 Tap **Transitions**.

The Transitions screen appears.

**15** Tap the transition you want.

**16** Tap **Slideshow Options**.

The Slideshow Options screen appears.

**17** If you want to play music during the slide show, tap the **Play Music** switch and move it to On.

The Music button appears.

**18** Tap **Music**.

The Music screen appears.

**19** Tap the song, album, or playlist you want to play.

The Slideshow Options screen appears again.

**20** Tap **Start Slideshow**.

The slide show starts.

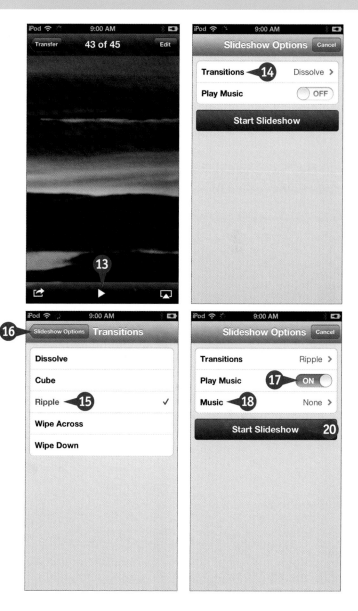

## TIP

**How can I play a custom slide show on the iPod touch?**

You cannot create a custom slide show on the iPod touch at this writing, so you need to set up the custom slide show beforehand. In iPhoto on a Mac, create an album or an event that contains the photos you want to show; in Windows, place the photos in a folder or create an album in an image-editing application. Use iTunes to sync the photos to your iPod touch. You can then open the group of photos and set it playing as a slide show.

# Play Photos from Your iPod touch on a TV

When you want to share your photos with other people, you can connect your iPod touch to a TV, and then display the photos on the TV screen. This is a great way to share the pictures at a size that a group of people can comfortably view.

To connect your iPod touch to a TV, you must get a cable with suitable connectors for the TV, such as the Apple Composite AV Cable or the Apple Component AV Cable. To play content, you must also set the iPod touch to provide the right type of video output for the TV.

## Play Photos from Your iPod touch on a TV

### Connect the iPod touch to the TV

First connect the Lightning connector on the TV cable to the iPod touch.

**Note:** To find the right kind of cable, check which type of input your TV uses.

Then connect the other end of the TV cable to the TV's port or ports.

### Choose Video Output Settings

 Press the Home button.

The Home screen appears.

 Tap **Settings**.

The Settings screen appears.

3 Tap **General**.

The General screen appears.

4 Tap **TV Out**.

**Note:** The TV Out item appears only when you have connected the iPod touch to a TV.

The TV Out screen appears.

 Tap the **Widescreen** switch and move it to On or Off, as needed for the TV.

 Tap **TV Signal**.

The TV Signal screen appears.

**7** Tap **NTSC** or **PAL**, as needed for the TV. See the tip for advice on which to choose.

**8** Tap **TV Out**.

**9** Press the Home button.

The Home screen appears.

## Play Photos on the TV

**1** Press the Home button.

The Home screen appears.

**2** Tap **Photos**.

The Photos screen appears.

**3** Locate the photos for the slide show. For example, tap **Albums**, and then tap the album.

The photos appear.

**4** Tap the photo you want to display first.

The photo appears on the TV. You can then display further photos by swiping a finger to the left or right.

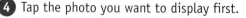

---

**TIP**

**Should I choose NTSC or PAL on the TV Signal screen?**
Normally, you need to choose the setting for the geographical area in which you are using the TV or from which the TV came. Most TV sets in North America use the NTSC format. Most TV sets in Europe use the PAL format. If in doubt, consult your TV's documentation.

# Read Digital Books with iBooks

To enjoy electronic books, or *e-books*, on your iPod touch, download the free iBooks app from the App Store. Using iBooks, you can read e-books that you load on the iPod touch from your computer, download free or paid-for e-books from online stores, or read PDF files you transfer from your computer.

If you have already loaded some e-books, you can read them as described in this task. If iBooks contains no books, see the next task, "Browse and Buy Digital Books with iBooks," for instructions on finding and downloading e-books.

## Read Digital Books with iBooks

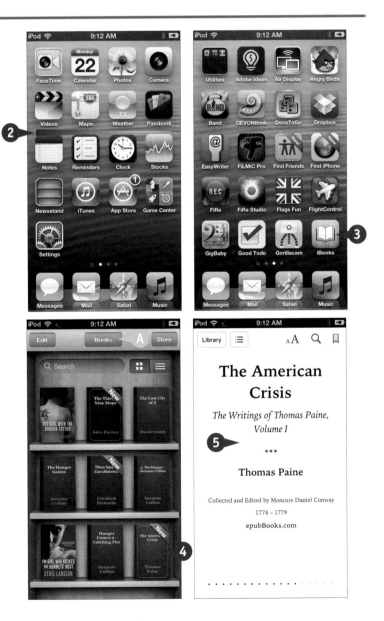

**1** Press the Home button.

The Home screen appears.

**2** Navigate to the Home screen that contains the iBooks icon. For example, tap and drag left to scroll to the right one or more times.

**3** Tap **iBooks**.

The Books screen appears.

**Ⓐ** If the Books button does not appear in the upper middle area of the iBooks screen, tap the button that appears there. On the Collections screen that appears, tap **Books** to display the Books screen.

**4** Tap the book you want to open.

The book opens.

**Note:** When you open a book, iBooks displays your current page. When you open a book for the first time, iBooks displays the book's cover or first page.

**5** Tap anywhere on the screen to hide the reading controls.

The reading controls disappear.

**Note:** To display the reading controls again, tap anywhere on the screen.

 Tap the right side of the page to display the next page.

**Note:** To display the previous page, tap the left side of the page. Alternatively, tap the left side of the page and drag to the right.

**7** To look at the next page without fully revealing it, tap the right side and drag to the left. You can then either drag further to turn the page or release the page and let it fall closed.

**8** To jump to another part of the book, tap **Table of Contents** ( ≡ ).

**Note:** Alternatively, you can drag the indicator at the bottom of the screen.

**9** When the table of contents appears, tap the part of the book you want to display.

**10** To search in the book, tap **Search** ( ⚲ ).

**11** On the Search screen, type the search term.

**12** Tap the match you want to display.

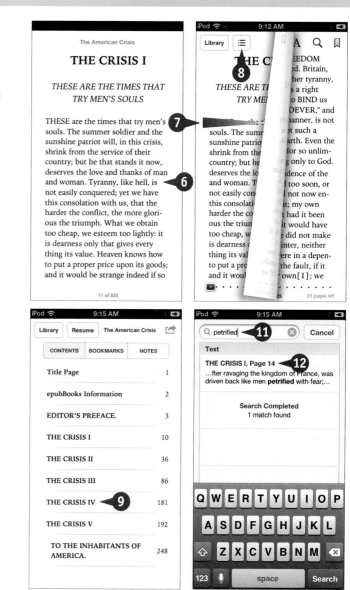

---

TIP

**How do I change the font iBooks uses?**

Tap the screen to display the controls, and then tap **Font Settings** ( ᴀA ). In the Font Settings dialog, tap **Small** (Ⓐ) or **Large** (Ⓑ) to change the font size. Tap **Fonts** (Ⓒ) to display the font list, and then tap the font you want to use. Finally, tap outside the Font Settings dialog to close it.

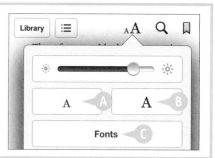

# Browse and Buy Digital Books with iBooks

The iBooks app connects directly Apple's online bookstore, which you can browse to find e-books. Some e-books are free; others you have to pay for, but many have samples that you can download to help you decide whether to buy the book.

After you download an e-book, it appears on your iBooks bookshelf. You can then open it and read it as described in the preceding task, "Read Digital Books with iBooks."

## Browse and Buy Digital Books with iBooks

**1** Open iBooks as described in the preceding task.

**2** Tap **Store**.

The Store screen appears.

**3** Tap **Books**.

The Books screen appears, showing the first part of each of several different lists of books — for example, New & Noteworthy and What's Hot.

**4** Tap **Categories**.

The Categories screen appears.

**5** Tap and drag up to scroll down the screen if necessary.

**6** Tap the category you want to view. For example, tap **History**.

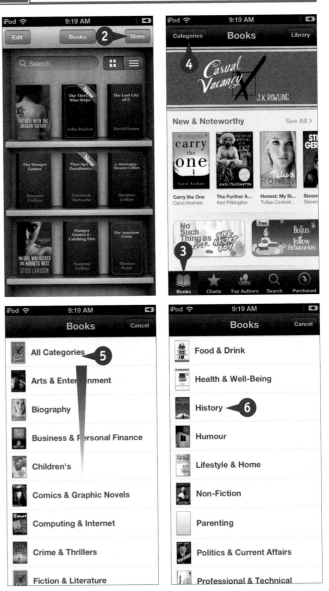

The screen appears for the category you chose.

**7** Tap **Charts**.

The Charts screen appears.

**Ⓐ** From the Charts screen, you can tap **Categories** to display the Categories screen, and then tap the category whose chart you want to see.

**8** Tap the book whose information you want to view.

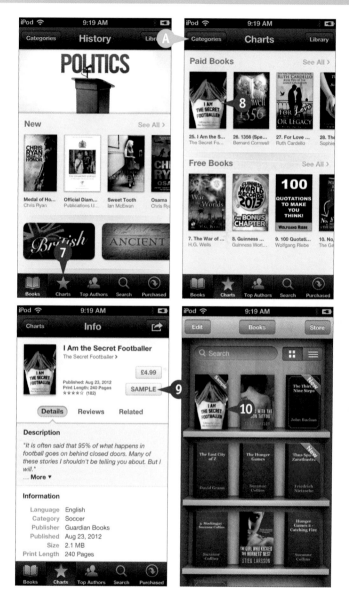

The book's screen appears.

**9** Tap **Sample** to get a sample of the book, or tap the price button to buy the book.

The sample or book appears on your iBooks bookshelf.

**10** Tap the sample or book to open it.

TIP

**Where can I find free e-books to read in iBooks?**

Open iBooks as described in the previous task. Tap **Browse** in the button bar at the bottom of the iBooks screen, and then tap **Top Free** to display an alphabetical list of authors by whom free books are available.

Other sources of free e-books include ManyBooks.net (www.manybooks.net) and Project Gutenberg (www.gutenberg.org).

# Add PDF Files to iBooks and Read Them

These days, many books, reports, and other documents are available as Portable Document Format files, or PDF files. You can load PDF files on your iPod touch and read them using iBooks. This is a great way to take your required reading with you so that you can catch up on it anywhere.

## Add PDF Files to iBooks and Read Them

### Add PDFs to iBooks Using iTunes

**1** Connect your iPod touch to your computer via the USB cable or Wi-Fi.

The iPod touch appears in the Devices list in iTunes.

**2** Click your iPod touch in the Devices list.

The iPod touch's control screens appear.

**3** Click **Books**.

The Books screen appears.

**4** Click the **File** menu.

The File menu opens.

**5** Click **Add to Library**.

The Add To Library dialog opens.

**6** Click the PDF file or select the PDF files you want to add.

**7** Click **Open**.

iTunes adds the PDF file or files to the Books list.

**8** Click **Sync**.

iTunes syncs the PDF files to the iPod touch.

**9** Disconnect the iPod touch from your computer.

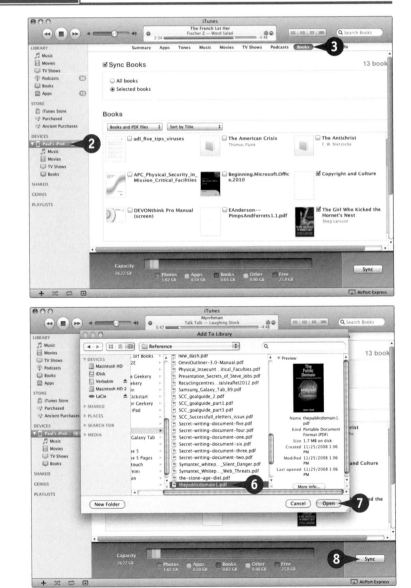

## Read a PDF File Using iBooks

**1** Press the Home button.

The Home screen appears.

**2** Navigate to the Home screen that contains the iBooks icon. For example, tap and drag left to scroll to the right one or more times.

**3** Tap **iBooks**.

The Books screen appears.

**4** Tap **Books**.

The Collections screen appears.

**5** Tap **PDFs**.

The PDFs screen appears.

**6** Tap the PDF file you want to open.

The PDF file appears. You can then read the PDF file using the techniques described earlier in this chapter.

**Note:** If you open a PDF file while browsing the web in Safari, you can open the file in iBooks. To do so, tap the screen, and then tap **Open in iBooks** on the command bar that pops up.

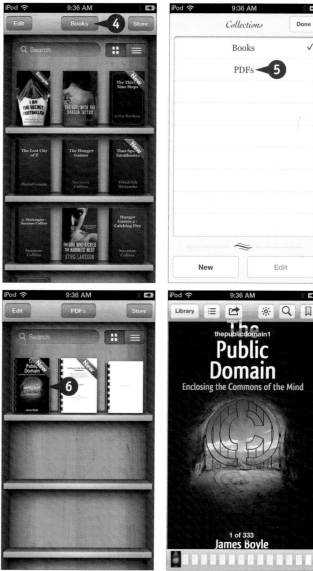

### How do I change the font size on the PDF file?

You cannot change the font size on the PDF file. This is because PDF is a graphical format — essentially a picture — instead of a text format. To make the PDF file more readable on the iPod touch, rotate the iPod touch to a landscape orientation, so that the screen is wider than it is tall. Then pinch outward to zoom the text to a larger size.

# CHAPTER 12

# Using Apps, Facebook, and Twitter

**Your iPod touch comes with apps that enable you to make the most of its features right out of the box.**

# Find Your Location with the Maps App

Your iPod touch's Maps app can pinpoint your location by using wireless networks. You can view your location on a road map, a satellite picture, or a hybrid that shows street annotations on the satellite picture. You can easily switch among map types to find the most useful one for your current needs.

## Find Your Location with the Maps App

 **1** Press the Home button.

The Home screen appears.

**2** Tap **Maps**.

The Maps screen appears.

**A** A blue dot shows your current location. The expanding circle around the blue dot shows that Maps is determining your location.

**Note:** It may take a minute for Maps to work out your location accurately. While Maps determines the location, the blue dot moves, even though the iPod touch remains stationary.

**3** Tap and pinch in with two fingers.

**Note:** You can tap and pinch out with two fingers to zoom in.

The map zooms out, showing a larger area.

**4** Tap the curled map corner.

The screen of map options appears.

**5** Tap **Satellite**.

The Satellite view appears.

**6** Tap the curled map corner.

The screen of options appears.

**7** Tap **Hybrid**.

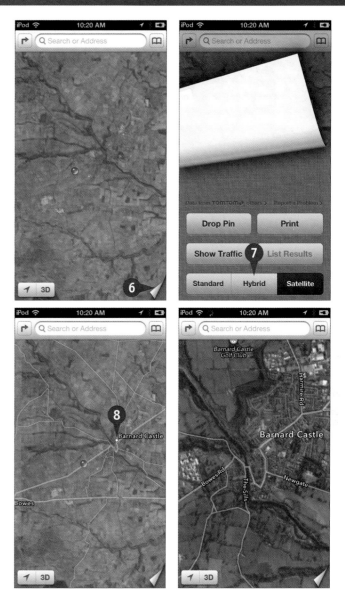

The satellite map appears with road names and place names overlaid on it.

**8** Double-tap an area of interest on the map.

Maps zooms in on the area you tapped.

---

**TIP**

**What does the 3D button in the lower-left corner of the Maps app do?**
Tapping **3D** ( **3D** ) switches the map to Flyover view, which enables you to zoom over the map. You learn to use Flyover view later in this chapter.

# Find Directions with the Maps App

Your iPod touch's Maps app can give you directions to where you want to go. Maps can also show you current traffic congestion to help you identify the most viable route for a journey.

Maps displays driving directions by default, but you can also display public transit directions and walking directions.

## Find Directions with the Maps App

**1** Press the Home button.

The Home screen appears.

**2** Tap **Maps**.

The Maps screen appears.

**3** Tap ➦.

The Directions screen appears.

**4** Tap **Start**.

The Current Location text changes to a blue button.

**5** Tap ⊗ to delete the Current Location button.

**Note:** If you want the directions to start from your current location, leave Current Location in the Start box. Skip to step **7**.

**6** Type the start location for the directions.

**Note:** If the starting location or ending location is an address in the Contacts app, start typing the name, and then tap the match in the list.

**7** Type the end location.

**A** Tap **Switch Places** (⟳) to switch the start location and end location.

**8** Tap **Route**.

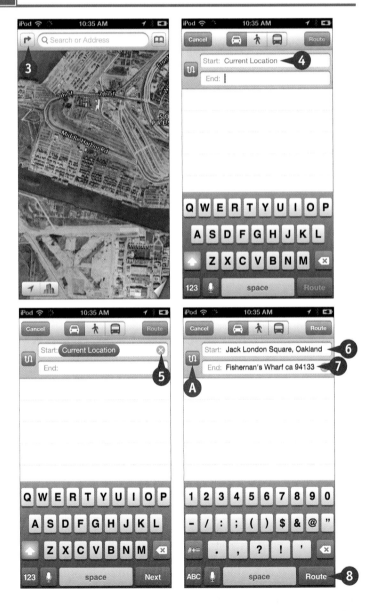

**B** A screen showing the driving directions appears. The green pin marks the start, and the red pin marks the end.

**Note:** If multiple routes are available, tap a button to view a different route. For example, tap **Route 2** ( Route 2 changes to Route 2 ) to view it.

**9** Tap **Start**.

The first screen of directions appears.

**10** Tap and scroll as needed to follow the directions.

The next screen of directions appears.

**11** Tap **Overview**.

The overview screen appears.

**12** Tap **Directions** ( ≣ ).

The Directions screen appears, showing a complete list of the directions.

**TIP**

**How do I get directions for public transit or walking?**

Tap 🚌 to display the details of available public transport. Tap 🚶 to display the distance and time for walking the route.

It is a good idea to double-check public transit directions against the latest published schedules, because the information is sometimes out of date.

Be aware that walking directions may be inaccurate. Before walking the route, check that it does not send you across pedestrian-free bridges or through rail tunnels.

# Explore with 3D Flyovers

Maps is not only great for finding out where you are and for getting directions to places, but it can also show you 3D flyovers of the places on the map.

After switching on the 3D feature, you can zoom in and out, pan around, and move backward and forward.

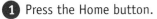

## Explore with 3D Flyovers

**1** Press the Home button.

The Home screen appears.

**2** Tap **Maps**.

The Maps screen appears.

**3** Display the area of interest in the middle of the screen. For example, tap and drag the map, or search for the location you want.

**4** Tap **3D** ( **3D** changes to **3D** ).

The screen switches to 3D view.

**5** Pinch out with two fingers to zoom in.

**Note:** You can pinch in with two fingers to zoom out.

**6** Tap and drag to scroll the map.

7 Place two fingers on the screen and twist clockwise or counterclockwise to rotate the view.

A The Compass arrow (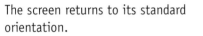) appears.

8 Tap 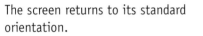.

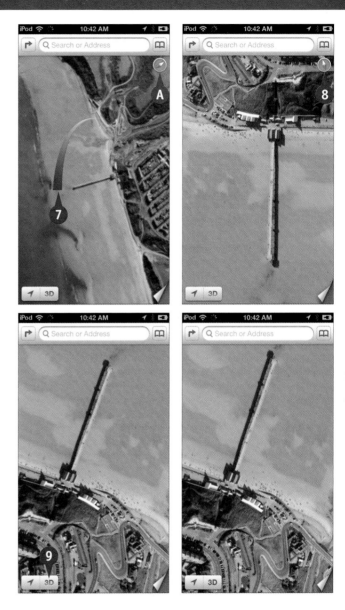

The screen returns to its standard orientation.

9 Tap **3D** (**3D** changes to **3D**).

The standard view reappears.

---

**TIP**

**What does Flyover do with the Standard map?**
When you tap **3D** to switch on Flyover with the Standard map displayed, Maps tilts the map at an angle, as you might do with a paper map. For most purposes, Flyover is most useful with the Satellite map and the Hybrid map.

# Use Maps' Bookmarks and Contacts

When you need to be able to return to a location easily in the Maps app, you can place a bookmark at the location.

Similarly, you can add a location to your contacts, so that you can access it either from the Contacts app or from the Maps app. You can either create a new contact or add the location to an existing contact.

You can also return quickly to locations you have visited recently but not created a bookmark or contact for.

## Use Maps' Bookmarks and Contacts

**1** Press the Home button.

The Home screen appears.

**2** Tap **Maps**.

The Maps screen appears.

**3** Find the place you want to bookmark. For example, tap and drag the map, or search for the location you want.

**4** Tap and hold the place you want to bookmark.

The Maps app drops a pin on the place.

**5** Tap ⦾.

The Location screen appears.

**6** At the bottom of the screen, tap **Add to Bookmarks**.

The Add Bookmark screen appears.

**7** Type the name for the bookmark.

**8** Tap **Save**.

**9** Tap **Add to Contacts**.

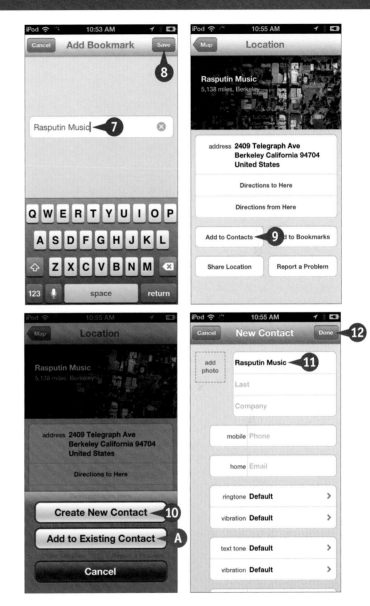

The Contact dialog opens.

**10** To create a new contact, tap **Create New Contact**.

The New Contact screen appears.

**A** To add the location to an existing contact, tap **Add to Existing Contact**, and then tap the contact on the All Contacts list.

**11** Type the details for the contact.

**12** Tap **Done**.

---

**TIP**

**How do I go to a location I have bookmarked or created a contact for?**

In the Maps app, tap **Bookmarks** ( 📖 ). On the Bookmarks screen, tap **Bookmarks** or **Contacts**, and then tap the location.

You can also go back to a recent location by tapping **Recents**, and then tapping the location.

| Bookmarks | Recents | Contacts |
|-----------|---------|----------|

Often, you will find it useful to share a location with other people. The Maps app enables you to share a location in moments via either e-mail or instant messaging.

You can share your current location, a location you have bookmarked or created a contact for, or a location on which you drop a pin.

## Share a Location via E-Mail and Instant Messaging

### Find the Location and Open the Share Dialog

 Press the Home button.

The Home screen appears.

② Tap **Maps**.

The Maps screen appears.

③ Find the location you want to bookmark.

④ If the location does not already have a bookmark or contact, tap and hold it to drop a pin on it.

⑤ Tap ⊙.

The Info screen appears.

Ⓐ If you have just dropped a pin, you may want to name it rather than leaving the default name, Dropped Pin. Tap **Add to Bookmarks**, type the name, and then tap **Done**.

⑥ Tap **Share Location**.

The Share dialog opens.

## Share the Location via E-Mail

 In the Share dialog, tap **Mail**.

Your iPod touch creates a new e-mail message in the Mail app with the location's link inserted in the message.

**2** Tap in the To box, and address the e-mail message.

**3** Tap in the Subject line, and type the subject for the e-mail message.

**4** Optionally, tap in the body area, and type any text needed.

**5** Tap **Send**.

## Share the Location via Instant Messaging

**1** In the Share dialog, tap **Message**.

Your iPod touch creates a new message in the Messages app with the location attached to the message.

**2** Tap in the To box, and address the message.

**3** Optionally, tap in the body area, and type any text needed.

**4** Tap **Send**.

### TIP

**How else can I share a location?**

You can also share a location on Twitter or Facebook. To share via Twitter, tap **Twitter**, type a suitable message on the Tweet screen, and then tap **Send**. To share via Facebook, tap **Facebook**, type any explanation needed, and then tap **Post**.

If you have created a contact for the location, you can share the contact from the Contacts app. Tap the contact's entry to display the Info screen, and then tap **Share Contact**. In the Share Contact Using dialog, tap **Email** or **Message**, as needed. You can then complete the message and send it.

# Track Stock Prices with the Stocks App

If you own or follow stocks, you can use the iPod touch's Stocks app to track stock prices so that you can take immediate action as needed.

The Stocks app displays a default selection of stock information at first, including the Dow Jones Industrial Average, the NASDAQ Composite, the Standard & Poor's 500, and Apple, Google, and Yahoo! stocks. You can customize the Stocks app to display only those stocks that interest you.

## Track Stock Prices with the Stocks App

### Open the Stocks App

‣ Press the Home button.

The Home screen appears.

‣ Tap **Stocks**.

The Stocks screen appears, showing a default selection of stocks.

### Choose the Stocks You Want to Track

**1** Tap **Info** (**ⓘ**).

The Stocks configuration screen appears.

‣ Tap **➕**.

The Search screen appears.

‣ Type the company's name or stock ID.

**4** Either tap **Search** or simply wait for the Stocks app to search.

A list of matching company names and stock symbols appears.

**5** Tap the item you want to add.

The stock listing appears.

**6** To remove a stock listing, tap ⊖.

**7** Tap the **Delete** button.

The stock listing disappears.

**8** To change the order, tap ≡ and drag up or down.

**9** Tap **%**, **Price**, or **Mkt Cap** to control which statistic the Stocks app displays first.

**10** Tap **Done**.

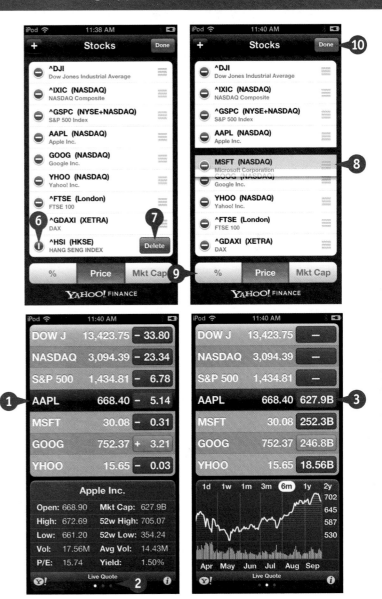

## View Information for a Stock

**1** On the Stocks screen, tap the stock for which you want to see information at the bottom of the screen.

**2** Tap the first dot to see the summary information, the second dot to see the stock chart, or the third dot to see stock-related headlines.

**Note:** You can also scroll the lower part of the screen to switch among the summary information, the stock chart, and the headlines.

**3** Tap to switch among percentage changes, price changes, and market capitalization.

---

Your iPod touch includes a powerful but straightforward Calculator app, a Voice Memos app for recording voice notes or audio, and a Clock app that has stopwatch and timer capabilities. The Newsstand app acts as a gateway to news and magazine apps.

## Use the Calculator App

Press the Home button to display the Home screen, and then tap **Utilities** to open the Utilities folder. Tap **Calculator** to open the Calculator app. You can then perform straightforward calculations in portrait orientation. For a fuller range of functions, turn your iPod touch to landscape orientation.

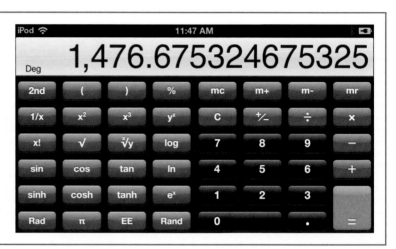

## Use the Voice Memos App

Press the Home button to display the Home screen, and then tap **Utilities** to open the Utilities folder. Tap **Voice Memos** to open the Voice Memos app. Tap ⬤ to start recording, and tap ⬤ to stop recording. Tap ⬤ to listen to the voice memo, share it, or delete it.

## Use the Stopwatch Feature in the Clock App

Press the Home button to display the Home screen, and then tap **Clock** to open the Clock app. Tap **Stopwatch** to display the Stopwatch screen, and then tap **Start** to start timing. Tap **Lap** to record a lap time, and tap **Stop** to stop timing. Tap **Reset** to reset the timer.

## Use the Timer Feature in the Clock App

Press the Home button to display the Home screen, and then tap **Clock** to open the Clock app. Tap **Timer** to display the Timer screen. Set the spin wheels to the countdown time, tap **When Timer Ends**, and then choose the sound to play. Tap **Start** to start the timer running.

## Use the Newsstand App

Press the Home button to display the Home screen, and then tap **Newsstand** to open the Newsstand. From here, you can tap a newspaper or magazine to open its app, or you can tap **Store** to visit the Newsstand store, where you can browse for newspapers and magazines. Tap an item to display its screen, and then tap **Free** or the price to download it to your iPod touch.

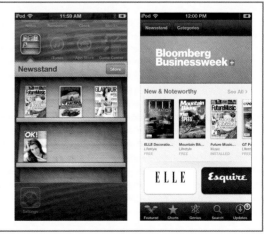

# Set Up the Clock App with Multiple Time Zones

When you travel, or when you work with people in different time zones, you may need to track the time in different time zones. You can set up your iPod touch's Clock app with the different time zones you need so that you can instantly see the local time in each time zone you need to track.

## Set Up the Clock App with Multiple Time Zones

**1** Press the Home button.

The Home screen appears.

**2** Tap **Clock**.

The Clock app appears.

**Note:** When you open the Clock app, it displays the last screen you used in the app.

**3** Tap **World Clock**.

The World Clock screen appears.

**4** Tap .

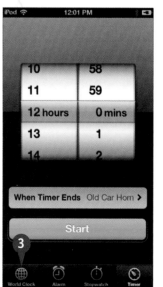

The Search screen appears.

**5** Type the city or time zone you want to find.

A list of matches appears.

**6** Tap the time zone you want to add.

The World Clock shows the clock you added.

**7** Tap **Edit**.

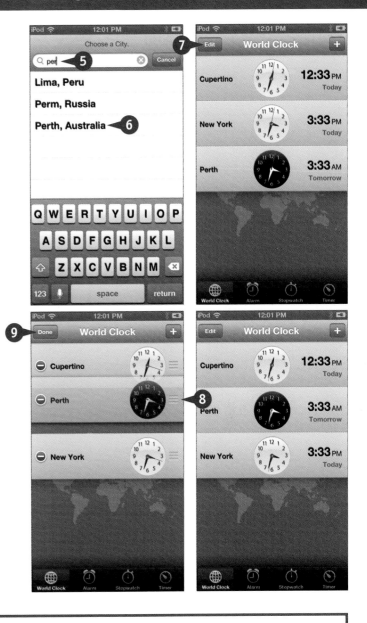

The World Clock screen opens for editing.

**8** Tap ≡ next to a clock, and drag it up or down the list as needed.

**Note:** To delete a clock, tap ⊖ next to it, and then tap **Delete**.

**9** Tap **Done**.

The clocks appear in your chosen order.

You can now easily see what time it is in each of the time zones you are tracking.

**Why do some clocks have black faces and others white faces?**

A black clock face indicates that it is currently between 6pm and 6am in that time zone. A white clock face indicates that it is between 6am and 6pm.

**How do I set the time on my iPod touch's main clock?**

Normally, your iPod touch sets the time automatically, but you can set the time manually if you want. From the Home screen, tap **Settings**, and then tap **General**. Tap **Date & Time**, and then use the controls on the Date & Time screen.

As well as showing the time in multiple locations, the Clock app includes full Alarm features. You can set as many alarms as you need, and create different schedules for the alarms — for example, you can set an alarm to wake you each weekday but not on the weekend.

## Set Alarms

**1** Press the Home button.

The Home screen appears.

**2** Tap **Clock**.

The Clock screen appears.

**3** Tap **Alarm**.

The Alarm screen appears.

**4** Tap ➕.

The Add Alarm screen appears.

**5** Tap the time controls to set the alarm time.

**6** To set a repeating alarm, tap **Repeat**.

The Repeat screen appears.

⑦ Tap to place a check mark next to each day you want the alarm to sound.

⑧ Tap **Back**.

The Add Alarm screen appears again.

⑨ Tap **Sound**.

The Sound screen appears.

⑩ Tap a sound to preview it.

A check mark appears next to the sound.

⑪ When you have chosen the alarm sound, tap **Back**.

The Add Alarm screen appears again.

⑫ Tap **Label**.

The Label screen appears.

⑬ Type the name for the alarm.

⑭ Tap **Done**.

The Add Alarm screen appears again.

⑮ Tap the **Snooze** switch, and move it to On or Off, as needed.

⑯ Tap **Save**.

The Alarm screen appears.

⑰ Move the alarm's switch to On or Off, as needed.

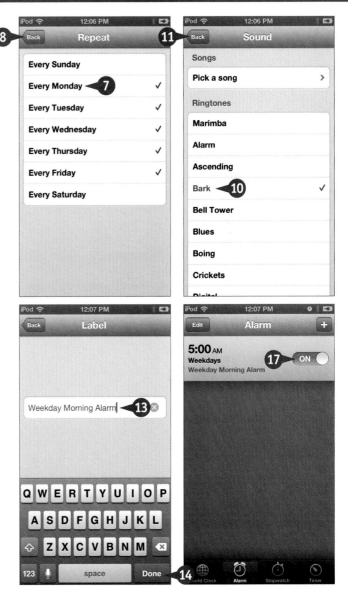

## TIP

**Is there an easy way to tell whether an alarm is set?**

Yes. The alarm icon (⏰) appears in the status bar when an alarm is set.

# Look Up Forecasts in Weather

Along with much other useful information, your iPod touch can put the weather forecasts in the palm of your hand. By using the Weather app, you can quickly learn the current conditions and forecast for as many cities as you need. The Weather app comes set to show the weather in Cupertino, the city where Apple's headquarters are located, but you can choose whichever cities you want. You can then move quickly from city to city as needed.

## Look Up Forecasts in Weather

### Open the Weather App and Add Your Cities

1 Press the Home button.

The Home screen appears.

2 Tap **Weather**.

The Weather app opens and displays the weather for either your current location or for Cupertino.

3 Tap **Info** ().

The Weather screen appears.

**Note:** To get local weather, you must allow Weather to use Location Services. On the Home screen, tap **Settings**, tap **Privacy**, and then tap **Location Services**. On the Location Services screen, tap the **Weather** switch and set it to On.

4 Tap ➕.

The Search screen appears.

5 Type the city you want to add.

6 Either tap **Search** or simply wait while the Weather app returns results.

7 Tap the result you want to add.

The Weather screen appears, showing the city you added.

**Note:** You can now add other cities as needed.

**8** Tap ≡, and drag a city up or down as needed.

**9** To delete a city, tap ⊖, and then tap **Delete**.

**10** Tap **Done**.

The Weather app displays the screen for the first city in the list.

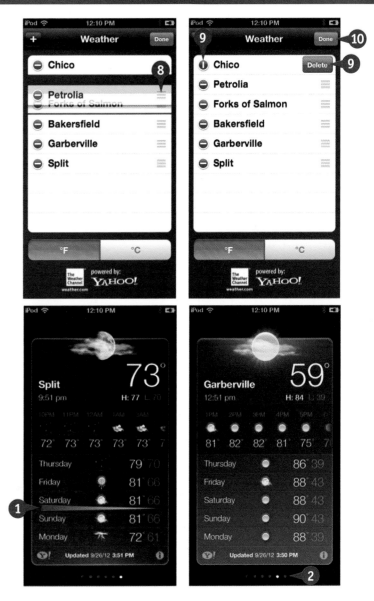

## Navigate from City to City

**1** Tap and drag to the left or the right.

The previous screen or next screen appears.

**2** Tap a dot to the left or right of the current dot.

The next screen in that direction appears.

| **TIPS** | |
|---|---|
| **How do I change from Centigrade to Fahrenheit?** Tap **Info** (ⓘ) to display the Weather screen, and then tap °**F** or °**C**, as needed. | **What does the Y! button in the Weather app do?** Tap the **Yahoo!** (🔘) button to display the Yahoo! Weather page for the current city in Safari. |

# Share Your Updates Using Twitter

**Y**our iPod touch's apps are fully integrated with Twitter, the online micro-blogging service. If you need to send a short textual tweet, you can use the Twitter app. If you need to send a photo, or share a still frame from a YouTube video, you can start from the Photos app or the YouTube app, and create a tweet in moments.

## Share Your Updates Using Twitter

### Send a Text Tweet

**1** Press the Home button.

The Home screen appears.

**2** Tap **Twitter**.

**Note:** If Twitter does not appear on the Home screen, tap **Settings**, tap **Twitter**, and then tap **Install**.

The Twitter app opens.

**3** Tap .

The New Tweet screen appears.

**4** Type the text of the tweet.

**Note:** You can also tap the microphone icon () to activate Siri, and then dictate the text of the tweet.

**5** Tap ✈ if you want to add your location to the tweet.

**6** Tap **Tweet**.

Twitter posts the tweet to your Twitter account.

## Send a Photo Tweet

**1** From the Home screen, tap **Photos**.

The Photos app opens.

**2** Navigate to the photo you want to tweet. For example, tap **Albums** and then tap the album that contains the photo.

**3** Tap the photo to display it.

**4** Tap ⬆.

The Share dialog appears.

**5** Tap **Twitter**.

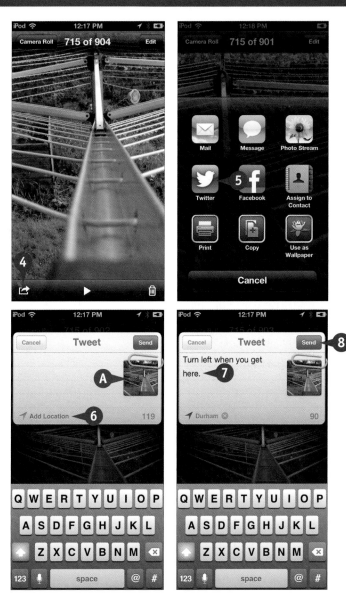

**A** The Tweet screen appears, showing the tweet with the photo attached.

**6** Tap **Add Location** if you want to add the location to the tweet.

**7** Type the tweet.

**8** Tap **Send**.

---

**TIP**

**How do I read other people's tweets?**

To read other people's tweets, use the Twitter app. Press the Home button to display the Home screen, tap **Twitter**, and then tap **Home** to catch up on tweets from the Twitter accounts you are following.

# Post Updates on Facebook

If you have an account on Facebook, the world's biggest social network, you can post updates directly from your iPod touch with a minimum of fuss.

You can work either from within the Facebook app or from apps that contain content suitable for Facebook posts. For example, you can post a photo from the Photos app to Facebook, as described in this task, or you can post a still frame from a YouTube video straight from the YouTube app.

## Post Updates on Facebook

### Post an Update Using the Facebook App

 Press the Home button.

The Home screen appears.

 Tap **Facebook**.

**Note:** If Facebook does not appear on the Home screen, tap **Settings**, tap **Facebook**, and then tap **Install**.

The Facebook app opens.

③ Tap **Status**.

The Update Status screen appears.

④ Type your update.

⑤ Tap **Post**.

Ⓐ The update appears on your screen.

## Post a Photo Update

 Press the Home button.

The Home screen appears.

 Tap **Photos**.

The Photos app opens.

3 Navigate to the photo you want to post. For example, tap **Albums** and then tap the album that contains the photo.

4 Tap the photo to display it.

5 Tap 🔗.

The Share dialog appears.

6 Tap **Facebook**.

The Facebook screen appears, with the photo ready for posting.

7 Type the text for the update.

8 Tap **Post**.

---

**TIP**

**From what other apps can I post updates to Facebook?**

You can post updates to Facebook from any app to which the developer has added Facebook integration. For example, you can post a location from the Maps app or a lecture from iTunes U to Facebook.

To see whether you can post updates to Facebook from an app, tap 🔗 from the app. If Facebook appears in the Share dialog, you can post an update to Facebook.

# CHAPTER 13

# Taking Photos and Videos

In this chapter, you begin by using the Camera app to take still photos, using the flash, the high dynamic range feature, and the panorama feature when needed. You then learn to capture video, edit videos using the Trim feature, and share both your photos and videos with others.

# Take Photos with the Camera App

Your iPod touch includes a high-resolution camera in its back for taking both still photos and videos, plus a lower-resolution camera in the front, for taking photos and videos of yourself and for making video calls.

To take photos using the camera, you use the Camera app. This app includes a digital zoom feature for zooming in and out, plus a flash that you can set to On, Off, or Auto.

## Take Photos with the Camera App

### Open the Camera App

**1** Press the Home button.

The Home screen appears.

**2** Tap **Camera**.

The Camera app opens. At first, the app shows a dark screen with shutter panels, which then open to display what is positioned in front of the lens.

### Compose the Photo and Zoom If Necessary

**1** Aim the iPod touch so that your subject appears in the middle of the photo area. If you need to focus on an item that is not in the center of the frame, tap the object to move the focus rectangle to it.

**Note:** If you need to take tightly composed photos, get a tripod that fits the iPod touch. You can find various models on eBay and photography sites.

**2** If you need to zoom in or out, place two fingers together on the screen and pinch outward.

The zoom slider appears.

**3** Tap ➕ to zoom in or ➖ to zoom out. Tap as many times as needed.

**Ⓐ** You can also zoom by tapping and dragging the zoom slider.

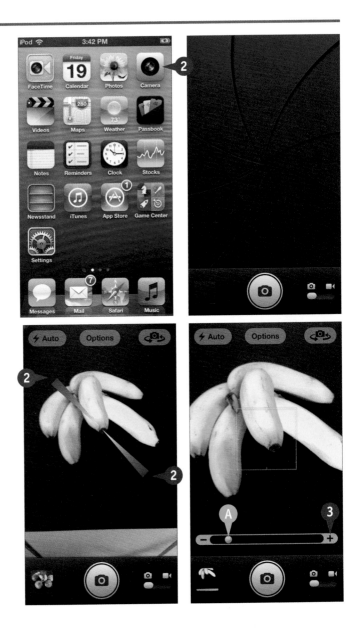

## Choose Whether and How to Use the Flash

 Tap the Flash button.

The Flash settings appear.

 Tap **On** to use the flash, **Auto** to use the flash if there is not enough light without it, or **Off** to turn the flash off.

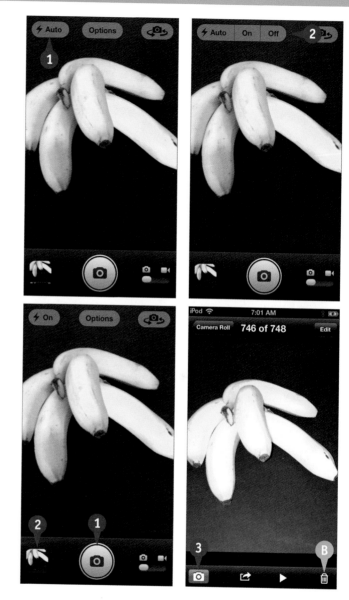

## Take the Photo and View It

① Tap **Take Photo** (  ).

The Camera app takes the photo and displays a thumbnail.

② Tap the thumbnail.

The photo appears.

Ⓑ From the photo screen, you can navigate as discussed in Chapter 11. For example, swipe your finger to the left to display the next photo, or swipe to the right to display the previous photo. Tap 🗑 to delete the photo.

③ Tap **Camera** ( ◎ ) when you want to go back to the Camera app.

**TIP**

**How do I switch to the front-facing camera?**

Tap **Switch Cameras** ( ⟳ ) to switch from the rear-facing camera to the front-facing camera. The image that the front-facing camera is seeing appears on-screen, and you can take pictures as described in this task. Tap **Switch Cameras** ( ⟳ ) again when you want to switch back to the rear-facing camera.

# Take HDR Photos and Panorama Photos and Use the Grid

The Camera app includes a feature called *high dynamic range*, or HDR. HDR takes three photos in immediate succession with slightly different exposure settings, and then combines them into a single photo that has a better color balance and intensity than a single photo.

To take an HDR photo with your iPod touch, you turn on the HDR feature in the Camera app, and then take the photo as normal. The Camera app also has a Grid feature that you can turn on to help you compose your pictures and a panorama mode for capturing landscapes.

## Take HDR Photos and Panorama Photos and Use the Grid

### Open the Camera App

**1** Press the Home button.

The Home screen appears.

**2** Tap **Camera**.

The Camera app opens. At first, the app shows a dark screen with shutter panels, which then open to display what is positioned in front of the lens.

### Turn On the HDR Feature

**1** Tap **Options**.

 The Options pop-up panel appears.

**Note:** You cannot use the HDR feature together with flash. So when you turn HDR on, your iPod touch automatically turns the flash off; when you turn the flash on, your iPod touch turns HDR off.

**2** Tap the **Grid** switch and move it to On if you want to display the Grid.

**3** Tap the **HDR** switch and move it to On to make the Camera app use HDR.

**Note:** The Grid is helpful both for making sure your subject is positioned suitably and for checking that you are holding the iPod touch so that uprights run vertically and horizontal items run horizontally.

**4** Tap **Done**.

The Options pop-up panel closes.

## Take the HDR Photo and View It

**1** If you turned on the grid, use it to position your subject and align the iPod touch.

**2** Tap **Take Photo** (  ).

The Camera app takes the photo, displaying Saving HDR and a wait symbol as it does so.

When the Camera app finishes taking the photo, it displays a thumbnail.

**3** Tap the thumbnail.

The second version of the photo appears.

**Note:** Swipe your finger left to display the first version of the photo.

**4** Tap **Camera** (  ) when you want to return to the Camera app.

**Note:** HDR combines three differently exposed photos into a single picture. It also saves the normal version of the photo — a version with a single exposure. If you do not want to save the normal version, turn off saving the normal version as described in the tip.

## TIP

**How do I take panorama photos?**

Tap **Options**, and then tap **Panorama**. Hold the iPod touch in portrait orientation, aim at the left end of the panorama, and then tap **Take Photo**. Follow the on-screen prompts to move the iPod touch to the right, keeping the white arrow on the blue horizontal line. Tap **Done** when you finish.

Move iPod continuously when taking a Panorama.

# Capture Video

As well as capturing still photos, your iPod touch's camera can capture high-quality, full-motion video. To capture video, you use the Camera app. You launch the Camera app as usual, and then switch it to Video mode. After taking the video, you can view it on the iPod touch's screen.

## Capture Video

**1** Press the Home button.

The Home screen appears.

**2** Tap **Camera**.

The Camera screen appears, showing the image the lens is seeing.

**3** Tap the **Camera** switch and move it to Video.

The video image and video controls appear.

**Note:** If the still camera is zoomed out all the way when you switch to the video camera, the picture appears to zoom in. This is because the video camera uses a focal length longer than the wide-angle setting of the still camera.

**4** Aim the camera at your subject.

**A** If you need to use the flash for the video, tap the flash button, and then tap **Auto** or **On**. When you are shooting video, the flash is effective only at short range.

**5** Tap **Record** ().

232

**B** The camera starts recording, the Record button glows brighter red, and the time readout shows the time that has elapsed.

**6** To finish recording, tap **Record** ().

The Camera app stops recording and displays a thumbnail of the video's first frame.

**7** Tap the thumbnail.

The video appears.

**8** Tap **Play** (▶).

The video starts playing.

**9** Tap anywhere on the screen to display the video controls.

**Note:** If you want to trim the video, follow the procedure described in the next task before tapping **Done**.

**10** When you finish viewing the video, tap **Camera** (📷).

The Camera app appears again.

---

**TIP**

**What does the bar of miniature pictures at the top of the video playback screen do?**
The navigation bar gives you a quick way of moving forward and backward through the movie. Tap the vertical playhead bar, and then drag to the right or to the left until the movie reaches the part you want. You can use the navigation bar either when the movie is playing or when it is paused.

# Edit Video with the Trim Feature

When you capture video, you normally shoot more footage than you want to keep. You then edit the video down to keep only the footage you need.

The Camera app includes a straightforward Trim feature that you can use to trim the beginning and end of a video clip to where you want them. For greater precision in editing, or to make a movie out of multiple clips, you can use the iMovie app.

## Edit Video with the Trim Feature

① Press the Home button.

The Home screen appears.

② Tap **Camera**.

The Camera screen appears, showing the image the lens is seeing.

③ Tap the **Camera** switch and move it to Video.

④ Tap the thumbnail.

The photos and videos in the Camera Roll appear.

**Note:** If the latest photo appears, tap **Camera Roll** to display the Camera Roll photos and videos.

⑤ Tap **Videos**.

The videos appear.

⑥ Tap the thumbnail for the video you want to trim.

The video opens.

⑦ Tap the left handle and drag it to the right.

The trim handles and the bottom of the navigation bar turn yellow to indicate that they are active.

⑧ Stop dragging when the frame appears where you want to trim the clip.

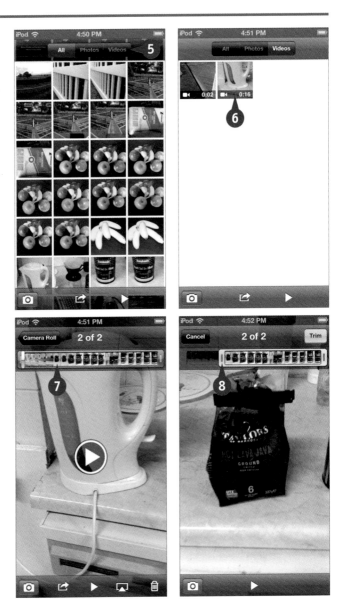

**9** Tap the right handle and drag it to the left until the frame to which you want to trim the end appears.

**10** Tap **Trim**.

The Trim dialog appears.

**11** Tap **Trim Original** if you want to trim the original clip. Tap **Save as New Clip** to create a new clip from the trimmed content, leaving the original clip unchanged.

**A** The Trimming Video progress indicator appears while the Camera app trims the video.

**12** Tap **Camera** (📷).

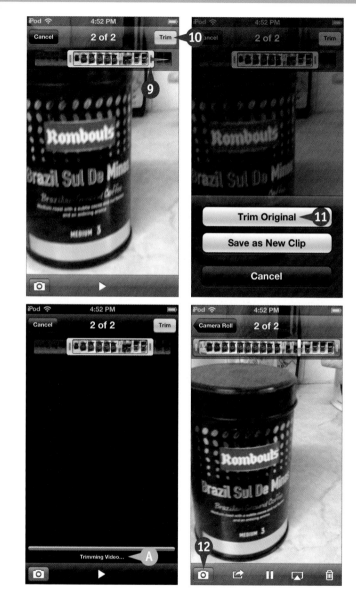

**Is there an easier way of trimming my videos?**

If you need to trim your videos on your iPod touch, try turning the iPod touch to landscape orientation. This makes the navigation bar longer and the trimming handles easier to use.

If you have a Mac, you can trim your videos more precisely, and make many other changes, by importing the clips into iMovie on the Mac, and then working with them there.

# Share Your Photos and Videos

After taking photos and videos with your iPod touch's camera, or after loading photos and videos on the iPod touch using iTunes, you can share them with other people.

Chapter 11 explains how to share photos via e-mail and MMS. This task explains how to tweet photos to your Twitter account, assign photos to contacts, use photos as wallpaper, or print photos.

## Share Your Photos and Videos

### Select the Photo or Video to Share

1. Press the Home button.

2. On the Home screen, tap **Photos**.

3. On the Photos screen, tap the item that contains the photo or video you want to share. For example, tap an album.

4. Tap the photo or video you want to share.

5. Tap **Share** (🖼) to open the Share dialog for photos or the Share dialog for videos.

### Share a Photo on Twitter

1. In the Share dialog, tap **Twitter**.

2. Type the text of the tweet.

3. Tap **Add Location** if you want to add your location to the tweet.

4. Click **Send**.

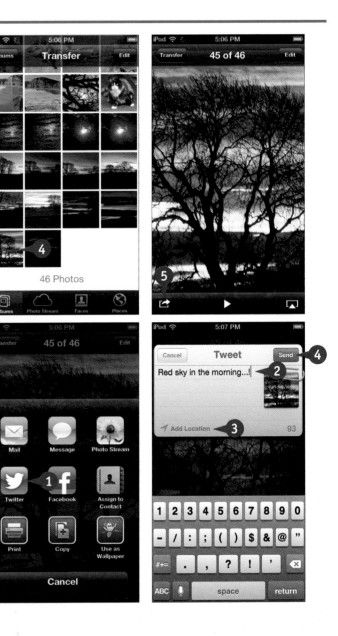

## Assign a Photo to a Contact

**1** In the Share dialog, tap **Assign to Contact**.

The list of contacts appears.

**2** Tap the contact you want to assign the photo to.

The Move and Scale screen appears.

**3** Move the photo so that the face appears centrally.

**4** If necessary, pinch in to shrink the photo or pinch out to enlarge it.

**5** Tap **Choose**.

## Set a Photo as Wallpaper

**1** In the Share dialog, tap **Use as Wallpaper**.

The Move and Scale screen appears.

**2** Move the photo to display the part you want.

**3** If necessary, pinch in to shrink the photo or pinch out to enlarge it.

**4** Tap **Set**.

The Set Wallpaper dialog appears.

**5** Tap **Set Lock Screen**, **Set Home Screen**, or **Set Both**, as needed.

**TIP**

**How do I print a photo?**

Display the photo you want to print, and then tap **Share** () to display the Share dialog. Tap **Print** to display the Printer Options screen. If the Printer readout does not show the correct printer, tap **Select Printer**, and then tap the printer. Tap **Print** to print the photo.

# CHAPTER 14

# Advanced Features and Troubleshooting

Your iPod touch includes advanced accessibility features. To keep your iPod touch running well, you should learn essential troubleshooting moves.

# Connect to a Network via VPN

I f you use your iPod touch for work, you may need to connect it to your work network. By using the settings, username, and password that the network's administrator provides, you can connect via virtual private networking, or VPN, across the Internet. You can also use VPN to connect to your home network if you set up a VPN server on it.

VPN uses encryption to create a secure connection across the Internet. By using VPN, you can connect securely from anywhere you have an Internet connection.

## Connect to a Network via VPN

### Set Up the VPN Connection on the iPod touch

**①** Press the Home button.

The Home screen appears.

**②** Tap **Settings**.

The Settings screen appears.

**③** Tap **General**.

The General screen appears.

**④** Tap **VPN**.

The VPN screen appears.

**⑤** Tap **Add VPN Configuration**.

**Note:** If your iPod touch already has a VPN you want to use, tap it, and then go to step **1** of the next section.

The Add Configuration screen appears.

**6** Tap the tab for the VPN type: **L2TP**, **PPTP**, or **IPSec**.

**7** Fill in the details of the VPN.

**8** Tap **Save**.

The VPN configuration appears on the VPN screen.

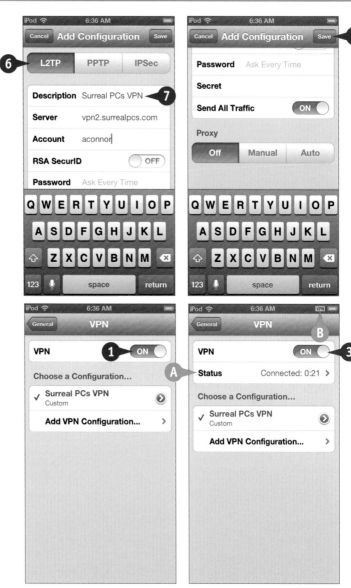

## Connect to the VPN

**1** On the VPN screen, tap the **VPN** switch and move it to On.

The iPod touch connects to the VPN.

**A** The Status readout shows Connected and the duration.

**B** The VPN indicator appears in the status bar.

**2** Work across the network connection as if you were connected directly to the network.

**3** When you are ready to disconnect from the VPN, tap the **VPN** switch on the VPN screen and move it to Off.

---

### TIP

**Is there an easier way to set up a VPN connection?**
Yes. An administrator can provide the VPN details in a file called a configuration profile. When you install the configuration profile — for example, by tapping the configuration profile in an e-mail message — your iPod touch adds the VPN automatically. You can then connect to the VPN.

# Connect Your iPod touch to Exchange Server

If your company or organization uses Microsoft Exchange Server, you can set up your iPod touch to connect to Exchange for e-mail, contacts, calendaring, and reminders.

Before setting up your Exchange account, ask an administrator for the details you need. These are your e-mail address, your password, the server name, and the domain name.

## Connect Your iPod touch to Exchange Server

**1** Press the Home button.

The Home screen appears.

**2** Tap **Settings**.

The Settings screen appears.

**Note:** If you have not yet set up an e-mail account on the iPod touch, you can also open the Add Account screen by tapping **Mail** on the iPod touch's Home screen.

**3** Tap and drag up to scroll down the screen until the fourth group of buttons appears.

**4** Tap **Mail, Contacts, Calendars**.

The Mail, Contacts, Calendars screen appears.

**5** Tap **Add Account**.

**6** On the Add Account screen, tap **Microsoft Exchange**.

**7** On the first Exchange screen, type your e-mail address.

**8** Type your password.

**9** Type a descriptive name for the account in the Description field.

**10** Tap **Next**.

The second Exchange screen appears.

**11** Type the server's address.

**12** Type the domain if needed.

**13** Type your username.

**14** Tap **Next**.

**15** On the next screen, tap the **Mail** switch and move it to On or Off, as needed.

**16** Tap the **Contacts** switch, and move it to On or Off, as needed.

**17** Tap the **Calendars** switch, and move it to On or Off, as needed.

**18** Tap the **Reminders** switch, and move it to On or Off, as needed.

**19** Tap **Save**.

**Is there an alternative way to set up an Exchange account?**

Yes. An administrator can provide the Exchange details in a configuration profile. If you have another e-mail account on your iPod touch, the administrator can send you the profile. Otherwise, you may need to download the profile from a web page. Either way, tap the file to install it.

**How do I know whether to enter a domain name when setting up my Exchange account?**

You need to ask an administrator because some Exchange implementations require you to enter a domain, whereas others do not.

# Use VoiceOver to Identify Items On-Screen

If you have trouble identifying the iPod touch's controls on-screen, you can use the VoiceOver feature to read them to you. VoiceOver changes your iPod touch's standard finger gestures so that you tap to select the item whose name you want it to speak, double-tap to activate an item, and flick three fingers to scroll.

VoiceOver can make your iPod touch easier to use. Your iPod touch also includes other accessibility features, which you can learn about in the next task.

## Use VoiceOver to Identify Items On-Screen

1 Press the Home button.

The Home screen appears.

2 Tap **Settings**.

The Settings screen appears.

3 Tap **General**.

The General screen appears.

4 Tap and drag up to scroll all the way down.

The bottom of the screen appears.

5 Tap **Accessibility**.

The Accessibility screen appears.

6 Tap **VoiceOver**.

**Note:** You cannot use VoiceOver and Zoom at the same time. If Zoom is on when you try to switch VoiceOver on, your iPod touch prompts you to choose which of the two to use.

**7** Tap the **VoiceOver** switch, and move it to On.

**8** Tap **VoiceOver Practice**.

A selection border appears around the button, and VoiceOver speaks its name.

**9** Double-tap **VoiceOver Practice**.

**10** Practice tapping, double-tapping, triple-tapping, and swiping. VoiceOver identifies each gesture and displays an explanation.

**11** Tap **Done** to select the button, and then double-tap **Done**.

**12** Swipe up with three fingers.

The screen scrolls down.

**13** Move the **Speak Hints** switch to On if you want VoiceOver to speak hints about using VoiceOver.

**14** Tap **Speaking Rate** to select it, and then swipe up or down to adjust the rate.

**15** Tap **Typing Feedback** to select it, and then double-tap.

**16** Tap the feedback type you want: **Nothing**, **Characters**, **Words**, or **Characters and Words**.

---

**TIP**

**Is there an easy way to turn VoiceOver on and off?**
Yes. You can set your iPod touch to toggle VoiceOver on or off when you press the Home button three times in rapid sequence. From the Accessibility screen, tap **Triple-click the Home Button for** to display the Triple-Click screen. Tap **VoiceOver** (Ⓐ), placing a check mark next to it, and then tap **Accessibility** (Ⓑ).

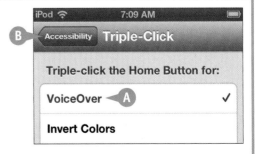

# Use Other Accessibility Features

VoiceOver can be helpful, but you probably also want to explore the other accessibility features that your iPod touch offers. These include zooming in the screen, displaying text at a larger size, changing the screen to reverse video, playing audio in mono, and speaking automatic corrections made while you type.

## Use Other Accessibility Features

**1** Press the Home button.

The Home screen appears.

**2** Tap **Settings**.

The Settings screen appears.

**3** Tap **General**.

The General screen appears.

**4** Tap and drag up to scroll all the way down.

The bottom of the screen appears.

**5** Tap **Accessibility**.

The Accessibility screen appears.

**6** Tap **Zoom**.

The Zoom screen appears.

**7** Tap the **Zoom** switch and move it to On.

**8** Double-tap the screen with three fingers to zoom in.

**9** Double-tap again with three fingers to zoom out.

**10** Tap **Accessibility**.

The Accessibility screen appears.

**11** Tap **Large Text**.

The Large Text screen appears.

**12** Tap the text size you want.

**13** Tap **Accessibility**.

The Accessibility screen appears.

**14** Tap the **Invert Colors** switch and move it to On.

The screen changes to reverse video.

**Note:** Tap the **Mono Audio** switch, and move it to On if you want to use mono audio.

**15** Tap the **Speak Auto-text** switch, and move it to On if you want your iPod touch to speak text corrections.

**16** Tap **General**.

### Is there an easy way to turn the Zoom feature on and off?

Yes. You can set your iPod touch to toggle Zoom on or off when you press the Home button three times in rapid sequence. From the Accessibility screen, tap **Triple-click the Home Button for** to display the Triple-Click screen. Tap **Zoom** (Ⓐ), placing a check mark next to it, and then tap **Accessibility** (Ⓑ). You can also use the Home triple-press to toggle the Invert Colors feature.

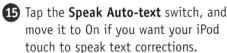

# Update Your iPod touch's Software

Apple periodically releases new versions of the iPod touch's software to fix problems, improve performance, and add new features. To keep your iPod touch running quickly and smoothly, and to add the latest features that Apple provides, you should update the iPod touch's software when a new version becomes available.

iTunes and your iPod touch notify you automatically when a new version of the iPod touch's software is available. You can also check manually for new versions of the software.

## Update Your iPod touch's Software

**1** Connect your iPod touch to your computer via the USB cable.

The iPod touch appears in the Devices list in iTunes.

A dialog appears telling you that a new software version is available.

**2** Click **Update**.

iTunes downloads the new software, extracts it, and begins to install it.

The Summary screen shows the progress of the installation.

**Ⓐ** If iTunes does not display the iPod touch's management screens, click the iPod touch in the Devices list to make the management screens appear.

When the installation is complete, iTunes displays a dialog telling you that the iPod touch will restart in 15 seconds.

**3** Click **OK**, or wait for the countdown to complete.

The iPod touch restarts, and then reappears in the Devices list in iTunes.

**4** Click your iPod touch in the Devices list.

The iPod touch's management screens appear.

**5** Verify the version number in the Software Version readout in the iPod box.

**6** Disconnect your iPod touch from the USB cable. You can now start using the iPod touch as usual.

**Your iPod has been updated, and is restarting. Please leave your iPod connected. It will appear in the iTunes window after it restarts.**

This message will be dismissed in 10 seconds.

OK

## TIPS

**How do I make iTunes check for a new version of my iPod touch's software?**

Connect your iPod touch to your computer via the USB cable so that the iPod touch appears in the Devices list in iTunes. When the Summary screen appears, click **Check for Update** in the Version box.

**Can I update my iPod touch's software without using a computer?**

Yes. You can update your iPod touch "over the air" by using a wireless network. Press the Home button, tap **Settings**, tap **General**, and then tap **Software Update** to check for new software.

To keep your iPod touch running all day long, you need to charge the battery fully by plugging the iPod touch into a USB socket, the Apple USB Power Adapter, or another power source. You can extend your iPod touch's runtime by reducing the demands on the battery. You can dim your iPod touch's screen so that it consumes less power. You can set your iPod touch to go to sleep quickly. You can turn off Wi-Fi and Bluetooth when you do not need them, and you can turn off location tracking when you do not need to track your iPod touch with the Find My iPod feature.

## Extend Your iPod touch's Runtime on the Battery

### Dim the iPod touch's Screen

❶ Press the Home button.

The Home screen appears.

❷ Tap **Settings**.

The Settings screen appears.

❸ Tap **Brightness & Wallpaper**.

The Brightness & Wallpaper screen appears.

❹ Tap the **Brightness** slider and drag it to the left to dim the screen.

❺ Tap **Settings**.

The Settings screen appears.

### Turn Off Wi-Fi and Bluetooth

❶ On the Settings screen, tap **Wi-Fi**.

The Wi-Fi screen appears.

❷ Tap the **Wi-Fi** switch and move it to Off.

❸ Tap **Settings**.

The Settings screen appears.

❹ Tap **Bluetooth**.

The Bluetooth screen appears.

**5** Tap the **Bluetooth** switch, and move it to Off.

**6** Tap **Settings**.

The Settings screen appears.

## Turn Off Location Tracking

**1** On the Settings screen, tap **Privacy**.

The Privacy screen appears.

**2** Tap **Location Services**.

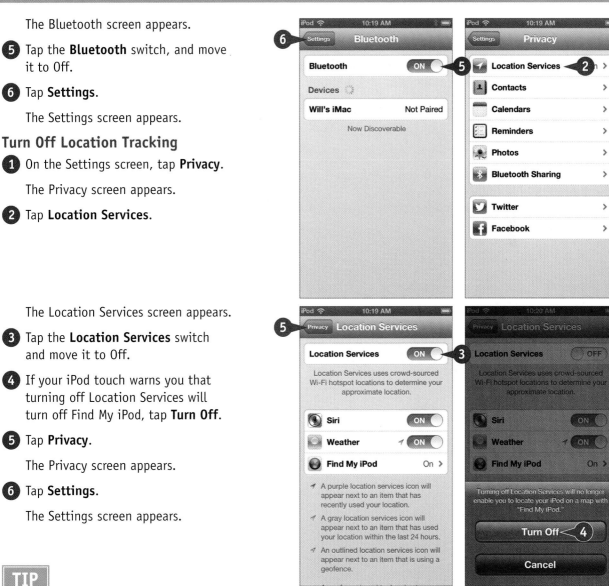

The Location Services screen appears.

**3** Tap the **Location Services** switch and move it to Off.

**4** If your iPod touch warns you that turning off Location Services will turn off Find My iPod, tap **Turn Off**.

**5** Tap **Privacy**.

The Privacy screen appears.

**6** Tap **Settings**.

The Settings screen appears.

## TIP

**How can I make my iPod touch put itself to sleep quickly?**
You can set a short time for the Auto-Lock setting. To do so, press the Home button. Tap **Settings**, tap **General**, and then tap **Auto-Lock**. Tap a short interval — for example, **1 Minute** (**Ⓐ**).

# Back Up and Restore Your iPod touch's Data and Settings with Your Computer

When you sync your iPod touch with your computer, iTunes automatically creates a backup of the iPod touch's data and settings. If your iPod touch suffers a software or hardware failure, you can restore the data and settings to your iPod touch. You can also sync your data and settings to a new iPod touch, an iPad, or an iPhone.

iTunes backs up the data that is unique on the iPod touch, such as the iPod touch's settings and notes you have created on the iPod touch, but does not back up music files, video files, or photos that you have synced to the iPod touch from your computer. For these types of files, which are still available on your computer, iTunes keeps a list of the files you have synced but does not keep extra copies of them.

## Back Up and Restore Your iPod touch's Data and Settings with Your Computer

① Connect your iPod touch to your computer via the USB cable or via Wi-Fi.

The iPod touch appears in the Devices list in iTunes.

② Click your iPod touch in the Devices list.

The iPod touch's management screens appear.

③ Click **Summary**.

The Summary screen comes to the front.

④ Control+click or right-click your iPod touch in the Devices list.

The context menu opens.

⑤ Click **Back Up**.

iTunes backs up your iPod touch.

⑥ Click **Restore**.

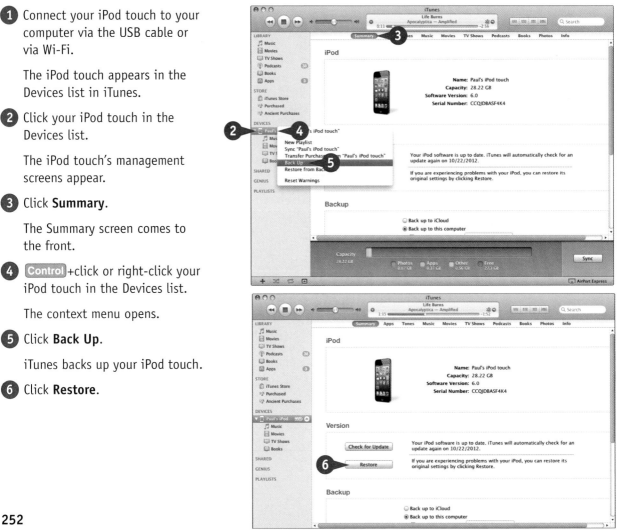

iTunes confirms that you want to restore the iPod touch to its factory settings.

**7** Click **Restore**.

iTunes backs up the iPod touch's data, restores the software on the iPod touch, and returns the iPod touch to its factory settings.

**Note:** Do not disconnect the iPod touch during the restore process. Doing so can leave the iPod touch in an unusable state.

iTunes displays the Set Up Your iPod screen.

**8** Click **Restore from the backup of** (○ changes to ◉ ).

**9** Click the pop-up menu, and choose your iPod touch by name.

**10** Click **Continue**.

iTunes restores the data and settings to your iPod touch.

Your iPod touch restarts, appears in the Devices list in iTunes, and then syncs.

**11** Disconnect the iPod touch.

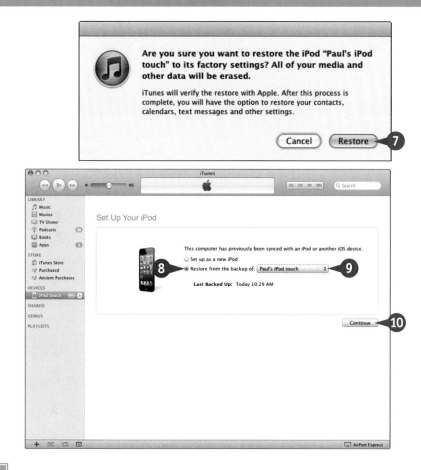

## TIP

**How can I protect confidential information in my iPod touch's backups?**
On the Summary screen in iTunes, click **Encrypt iPod touch backup** (☐ changes to ☑ ). In the Set Password dialog, type the password (**A**), and then click **Set Password** (**B**). iTunes then encrypts your backups using strong encryption.

# Back Up and Restore Your iPod touch's Data and Settings with iCloud

When you sync your iPod touch with iCloud, you create a backup of the iPod touch's data and settings in your storage area on iCloud. If your iPod touch suffers a software or hardware failure, you can restore the data and settings to your iPod touch. At this writing, a standard free iCloud account gives you 5GB of data storage. This is enough to store your iPod touch's settings and your most important data and files. You can buy more storage, but you must set your iPod touch to back up exactly those items you want to keep in iCloud. The iTunes Store lets you download again all the apps, media files, and games you have bought, so you do not need to back up these files.

## Back Up and Restore Your iPod touch's Data and Settings with iCloud

① Press the Home button.

The Home screen appears.

② Tap **Settings**.

The Settings screen appears.

③ Tap and drag up to scroll down the screen until the fourth box appears.

④ Tap **iCloud**.

The iCloud screen appears, showing the name of the iCloud account you have set up.

⑤ Choose the data you want to synchronize with iCloud by moving the Mail, Contacts, Calendars, Reminders, Bookmarks, and Notes switches to On or Off as needed.

⑥ If you need to buy more storage, tap your account name.

The Account screen appears, showing your storage amount in the Storage Plan area.

⑦ Tap the **Storage Plan** button.

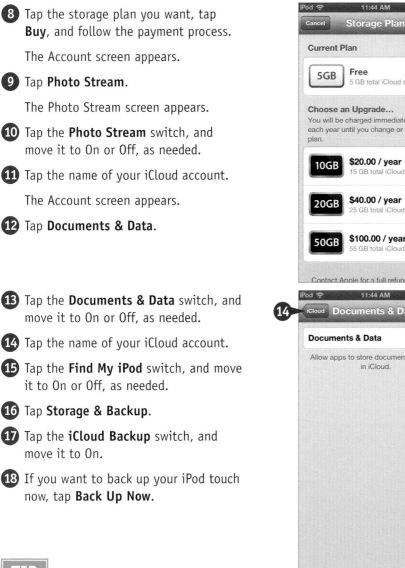

**8** Tap the storage plan you want, tap **Buy**, and follow the payment process.

The Account screen appears.

**9** Tap **Photo Stream**.

The Photo Stream screen appears.

**10** Tap the **Photo Stream** switch, and move it to On or Off, as needed.

**11** Tap the name of your iCloud account.

The Account screen appears.

**12** Tap **Documents & Data**.

**13** Tap the **Documents & Data** switch, and move it to On or Off, as needed.

**14** Tap the name of your iCloud account.

**15** Tap the **Find My iPod** switch, and move it to On or Off, as needed.

**16** Tap **Storage & Backup**.

**17** Tap the **iCloud Backup** switch, and move it to On.

**18** If you want to back up your iPod touch now, tap **Back Up Now**.

---

**TIP**

**How do I restore my iPod touch from its iCloud backup?**

First, reset the iPod touch to factory settings. Press the Home button, tap **Settings**, tap **General**, tap **Reset**, and tap **Erase All Content and Settings**. Tap **Erase iPod touch** in the confirmation dialog. When the iPod touch restarts and displays its setup screens, choose your language and country. On the Set Up iPod screen, tap **Restore from iCloud Backup**, and then tap **Next**. On the Apple ID screen, enter your Apple ID, and then tap **Next**. On the Choose Backup screen, tap the backup you want to use — normally, the most recent backup — and then tap **Restore**.

# Reset Your Network, Dictionary, and Home Screen Settings

After experimenting with changes to your iPod touch's settings, you may want to restore the iPod touch to the default settings to undo the changes you have made. For example, you may want to restore your Home screen to its default settings to undo customizations.

From the Reset screen, you can quickly reset your network settings, your keyboard dictionary, your Home screen layout, or your location warnings. You can also reset all settings, as discussed in the next task.

## Reset Your Network, Dictionary, and Home Screen Settings

**1** Press the Home button.

The Home screen appears.

**2** Tap **Settings**.

The Settings screen appears.

**3** Tap **General**.

The General screen appears.

**4** Scroll down all the way to the bottom.

The lower part of the General screen appears.

**5** Tap **Reset**.

The Reset screen appears.

**6** Tap **Reset Network Settings**, **Reset Keyboard Dictionary**, or **Reset Home Screen Layout**, as needed.

**Note:** Resetting the network settings deletes all network information you have entered, such as passwords for wireless networks. Resetting the keyboard dictionary deletes the custom words you have added to it. Resetting the Home screen layout puts the Home screen icons back in their default places.

A confirmation dialog opens, showing a brief explanation of what the command will reset.

**7** Tap the **Reset** button in the dialog.

The iPod touch resets the item you chose.

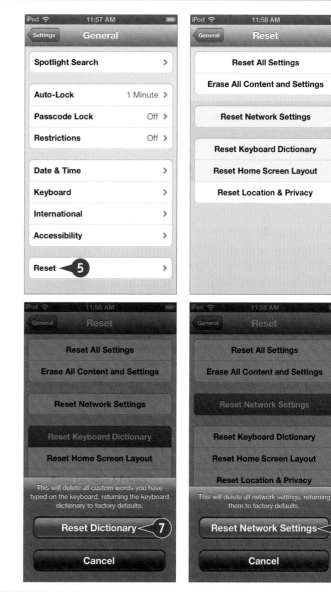

**What does the Reset Location Warnings button on the Reset screen do?**

When an app first requests location information, your iPod touch asks your permission. For example, when you first take a photo using the Camera app, the Camera app requests your location so that it can store it in the photo. After you tap **OK** (Ⓐ) for such a request, your iPod touch does not ask you again for the same app. Resetting the location warnings makes each app request permission again.

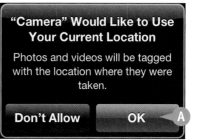

# Restore Your iPod touch to Factory Settings

If your iPod touch starts malfunctioning and you cannot get iTunes to recognize it, you may need to restore the iPod touch to factory settings. This is an operation you perform on the iPod touch itself when severe problems occur with its settings, to get the iPod touch into a state where it can communicate with iTunes again.

If iTunes can recognize the iPod touch, use iTunes to restore the iPod touch instead of resetting the iPod touch as described here.

## Restore Your iPod touch to Factory Settings

1 Press the Home button.

The Home screen appears.

2 Tap **Settings**.

The Settings screen appears.

**Note:** If your iPod touch is not responding to the Home button or your taps, press and hold the Sleep/Wake button and the Home button for about 15 seconds to reset the iPod touch.

3 Tap **General**.

The General screen appears.

4 Scroll down all the way to the bottom.

The lower part of the General screen appears.

**5** Tap **Reset**.

The Reset screen appears.

**6** Tap **Reset All Settings**.

**Note:** If you have applied a restrictions passcode to the iPod touch, you must enter the passcode after tapping Reset All Settings.

A confirmation dialog appears.

**7** Tap **Reset All Settings**.

A second confirmation dialog appears, because resetting all settings makes such a serious change to your iPod touch.

**8** Tap **Reset All Settings**.

The iPod touch resets all its settings.

**Does resetting all the iPod touch's settings delete my data and my music files?**
No, it does not. When you reset all the iPod touch's settings, the settings go back to their defaults, but your data remains in place. But you need to set the iPod touch's settings again, either by restoring them using iTunes or by setting them manually, in order to get your iPod touch working the way you prefer.

# Troubleshoot Wi-Fi Connections

To get the most out of your iPod touch and its powerful Internet features, use Wi-Fi networks whenever they are available.

Normally, the iPod touch establishes and maintains Wi-Fi connections without problems. But you may sometimes need to request your iPod touch's network address again, a process called renewing the lease on the IP address. You may also need to tell your iPod touch to forget a network, and then rejoin the network manually, providing the password again.

## Troubleshoot Wi-Fi Connections

### Renew the Lease on Your iPod touch's IP Address

 Press the Home button.

The Home screen appears.

2 Tap **Settings**.

The Settings screen appears.

3 Tap **Wi-Fi**.

The Wi-Fi screen appears.

4 Tap ⊙ to the right of the network for which you want to renew the lease.

The network's screen appears.

5 Tap **Renew Lease**.

The Renew Lease dialog opens.

6 Tap **Renew Lease**.

7 Tap **Wi-Fi Networks**.

The Wi-Fi screen appears.

## Forget a Network and Then Rejoin It

**1** On the Wi-Fi screen, tap ⊚ to the right of the network.

The network's screen appears.

**2** Tap **Forget this Network**.

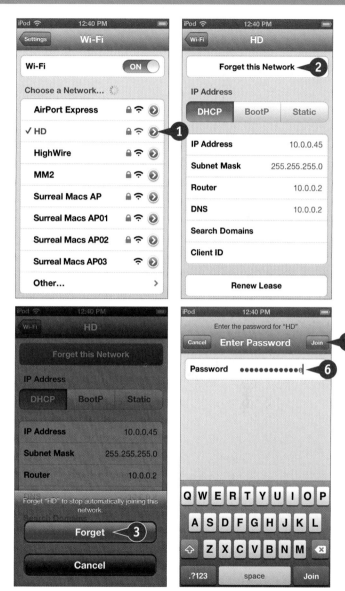

The Forget this Network dialog opens.

**3** Tap **Forget**.

The iPod touch removes the network's details.

**4** Tap **Wi-Fi Networks**.

The Wi-Fi screen appears.

**5** Tap the network's name.

The password screen appears.

**6** Type the password for the network.

**7** Tap **Join**.

The iPod touch joins the network.

---

**TIP**

### What else can I do to reestablish my Wi-Fi network connections?

If you are unable to fix your Wi-Fi network connections by renewing the IP address lease or by forgetting and rejoining the network, as described in this task, try restarting your iPod touch. If that does not work, reset your network settings, as described earlier in this chapter, and then set up each connection again manually.

# Troubleshoot iTunes Sync Problems

To keep your iPod touch charged and loaded with your current data and media files from your computer, connect it regularly to your computer and sync it using iTunes. Connection and syncing are usually straightforward, but you may sometimes find that iTunes does not recognize your iPod touch when you connect it. When this happens, you will have to troubleshoot the physical connection and iTunes' settings. If iTunes is not set to sync automatically with your iPod touch, you must start the sync manually.

## Troubleshoot iTunes Sync Problems

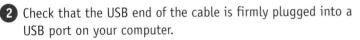

### Check the USB Connection between Your Computer and Your iPod touch

① Check that the Lightning connector end of the cable is firmly plugged into the Lightning port on the iPod touch. You may need to remove any case in order to make a good connection.

**Note:** Make sure the USB port you use is a full-power port rather than a low-power port. Use a USB port directly on your computer rather than a USB port on a hub or a peripheral device such as a keyboard.

② Check that the USB end of the cable is firmly plugged into a USB port on your computer.

### Restart the iPod touch

① Press and hold the Power/Sleep button on the iPod touch for several seconds.

② On the shutdown screen, tap and drag the slider to the right.

The iPod touch turns off.

③ Press and hold the Power/Sleep button for two seconds.

The Apple logo appears on the screen, and the iPod touch restarts.

④ Connect the iPod touch to your computer via the USB cable.

## Restart iTunes

**1** Close iTunes. In Windows, click **File** and then **Exit**. On a Mac, click **iTunes** and then **Quit iTunes**.

**Note:** If neither restarting your iPod touch nor restarting iTunes enables the two to communicate, try restarting your PC or Mac.

**2** Restart iTunes. In Windows, click the **iTunes** icon on the Start menu or Start screen. On a Mac, click the **iTunes** icon on the Dock.

**3** Connect the iPod touch to your computer via the USB cable.

## Verify Automatic Syncing or Start a Sync Manually

**1** If iTunes does not launch or become active when you connect your iPod touch, launch or activate iTunes manually.

**2** Click your iPod touch in the Devices list.

**3** On the iPod touch's management screen, click **Summary**.

**4** Click **Open iTunes when this iPod is connected** (☐ changes to ☑).

**5** Click **Apply**.

**TIP**

**Why does nothing happen when I connect my iPod touch to my computer?**
If your iPod touch's battery is exhausted, nothing happens for several minutes after you connect your iPod touch to your computer. This is because the iPod touch is charging its battery via the USB cable. After a few minutes, when the iPod touch's battery has enough charge to power the screen, the screen comes on, and syncing begins as usual.

# Locate Your iPod touch with Find My iPod

I f you have an iCloud account, you can use the Find My iPod feature to locate your iPod touch when you have lost it or it has been stolen. You can also display a message on the iPod touch — for example, to tell the person who has found the iPod touch how to contact you — or remotely wipe the data on the iPod touch.

To use Find My iPod, you must first set up your iCloud account on your iPod touch, and then enable the Find My iPod feature.

## Locate Your iPod touch with Find My iPod

### Turn On the Find My iPod Feature

1. Set up your iCloud account on your iPod touch as discussed in "Set Up Your Mail Accounts" in Chapter 5.

2. Press the Home button.

   The Home screen appears.

3. Tap **Settings**.

   The Settings screen appears.

4. Tap and drag up to scroll down the screen until the fourth box of buttons appears.

5. Tap **Mail, Contacts, Calendars**.

   The Mail, Contacts, Calendars screen appears.

6. Tap your iCloud account.

   The screen for your iCloud account appears.

7. Tap the **Find My iPod** switch, and move it to On.

   A confirmation dialog appears.

8. Tap **Allow**.

9. Tap **Mail, Contacts, Calendars**.

## Locate Your iPod touch Using Find My iPod

1. Open a web browser, such as Internet Explorer or Safari.

2. Click the Address box.

3. Type **www.icloud.com**, and press **Enter** in Windows or **Return** on a Mac.

   The iCloud Sign In web page appears.

4. Type your username.

5. Type your password.

6. Click ⊙.

   The iCloud site appears, displaying the page you last used.

7. Click **iCloud** (☁).

   The iCloud apps screen appears.

8. Click **Find My iPhone**.

**Is it worth displaying a message on my iPod touch, or should I simply wipe it?**

Almost always, it is definitely worth displaying a message on your iPod touch. If you have lost your iPod touch, and someone has found it, that person may be trying to return it to you. The chances are good that the finder is honest, even if he has not discovered that you have locked the iPod touch with a passcode. That said, if you are certain someone has stolen your iPod touch, you may prefer simply to wipe it, using the technique explained next.

continued ▶

Find My iPod is a powerful feature that you can use both when you have mislaid your iPod touch and when someone has deliberately taken it from you.

If Find My iPod reveals that someone has taken your iPod touch, you can wipe its contents to prevent whoever has taken it from hacking into your data. Be clear that wiping your iPod touch prevents you from locating the iPod touch again — ever — except by chance. Wipe your iPod touch only when you have lost it, you have no hope of recovering it, and you must destroy the data on it.

## Locate Your iPod touch with Find My iPod (continued)

The iCloud Find My iPhone screen appears.

**9** Click **Devices**.

**A** The My Devices panel appears.

**10** Click your iPod touch.

The Info dialog appears, showing the iPod touch's location.

**11** If you want to play a sound on the iPod touch, click **Play Sound**. This feature is primarily helpful for locating your iPod touch if you have mislaid it somewhere nearby.

**B** A message indicates that the iPod touch has played the sound.

### Lock the iPod touch with a Passcode

**1** Click **Lost Mode** in the Info dialog.

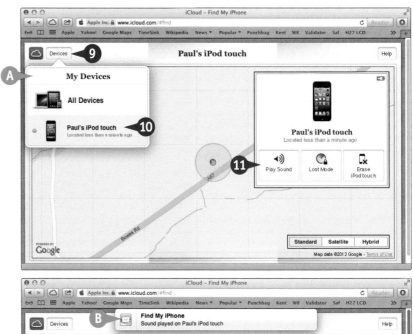

The Lost Mode dialog appears.

**2** Click the numbers for a new passcode to apply to the iPod touch.

The Lost Mode dialog displays its Re-enter Passcode screen.

**3** Click the passcode numbers again.

**4** Optionally, type a contact phone number.

**5** Click **Next**.

**6** Optionally, type a message to whoever finds your iPod touch.

**7** Click **Done**.

iCloud sends the lock request to the iPod touch, and then displays a panel telling you it sent the request.

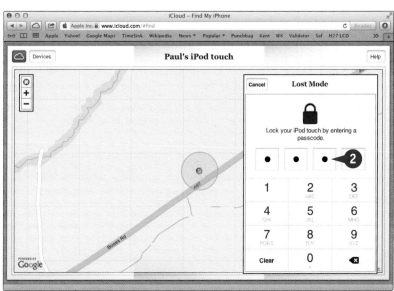

### Remotely Erase the iPod touch

**1** Click **Erase iPod touch** in the Info dialog.

The Enter Your Apple ID Password dialog appears.

**2** Type your password.

**3** Click **Erase**.

iCloud sends the erase request to the iPod touch, which erases its data.

---

## TIP

**Can I remotely erase the data on my iPod touch if I do not have an iCloud account?**
You can set a passcode for the iPod touch as discussed in Chapter 3, and then move the **Erase Data** switch on the Passcode Lock screen to On. This setting makes the iPod touch automatically erase its data after ten successive failed attempts to enter the passcode.

# Index

# S